Hiking
OREGON'S GEOLOGY

Hiking

OREGON'S GEOLOGY

ELLEN MORRIS BISHOP
and
JOHN ELIOT ALLEN

THE
MOUNTAINEERS

For Spirits Little Wolf
and all those who love wild places

Published by
The Mountaineers
1001 SW Klickitat Way
Seattle, WA 98134

All rights reserved
First edition: first printing 1996, second printing 1997

Published simultaneously in Canada by Douglas & McIntyre, Ltd., 1615 Venables Street, Vancouver, B.C. V5L 2H1

Published simultaneously in Great Britain by Cordee, 3a DeMontfort Street, Leicester, England, LE1 7HD

Manufactured in the United States of America

Edited by Kris Fulsaas
Maps by Warren Huskey
All photographs by Ellen Bishop unless otherwise specified
Cover design by Watson Graphics
Book design by Ani Rucki
Book layout by Gray Mouse Graphics

Cover photographs: Backdrop: *Eocene basaltic pillow lava forms much of Marys Peak, Oregon Coast Range.* Insets, left to right: *6500-year-old basalt flows frame Mount Jefferson, Cascade Mountains; Layered periodite near Vulcan Lake, Klamath Mountains; Welded tuffs bracket sculpted cliffs, Owyhee Mountains.*
Frontispiece: *View of Wizard Island and Mount Scott from The Watchman at Crater Lake*

Library of Congress Cataloging-in-Publication Data
Bishop, Ellen Morris.
    Hiking Oregon's geology / Ellen Morris Bishop and John Eliot Allen.
       p.   cm.
    Includes bibliographical references (p.   ) and index.
    ISBN 0-89886-485-2
    1. Hiking—Oregon—Guidebooks. 2. Geology—Oregon—Guidebooks. 3. Oregon—Guidebooks. I. Allen, John Eliot, 1908–   . II. Title.
GV199.42.07B57   1996
917.95—dc20   96–23999
                                                                     CIP

Contents

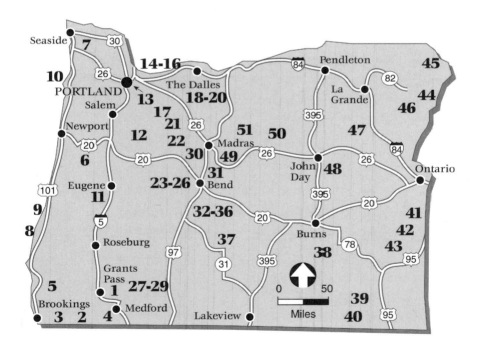

Hammer and compass are among a field geologist's most important tools.

Preface

This is a book about Oregon's geology for hikers and walkers and wanderers, and for all those who wonder about landscapes and time. It is a guide, not a textbook. This book is written primarily with the geologic layperson in mind. It enables me to share some of the places I know and love. And it helps the rocks tell their own tales, for, to my way of thinking, the best place to learn geology is running with the wild rocks, far from the confines of orderly cardboard boxes of sterile, tame stones branded with neat little numbers.

There are a few rules geologists must follow. They are mostly concepts of physics and chemistry and biology, ideas like plate tectonics, the physics of compression and pulling apart, the chemistry of crystallization and cooling. But within these bounds, anything is possible. Sometimes we deny the obvious because it challenges convention. When J Harlen Bretz proposed his hypothesis about the Missoula floods in 1923, he was spurned by nearly all his fellow scientists, whose imaginations dwelled in the straitjacket of belief. There are thousands of similar tales.

Laypeople can often figure things out just as well as geologic professionals. Several years ago I received a letter from a Seattle man who was building a dollhouse for his granddaughter. He noticed that when he hammered on a piece of plywood, the sawdust gathered in little mounds. Could shaking, perhaps by earthquakes, be the cause of the Mima Mounds south of Seattle, he wondered? A month later, in the scientific journal *Geology*, a very serious geophysicist proposed a genetic relation between the Mima Mounds and shaking due to earthquakes.

When I am on a barren outcrop, among my favorite things to do is close my eyes and imagine what it was like when this very rock I am sitting on was formed. With very little effort, I can transport myself from a Wallowa Mountain peak to a tropical island, or from the dusty Painted Hills to a verdant lake where miniature horses graze and rhinos wade. I can sit on the outcrop and listen to lava sizzle, or visit Silver Falls and hear ocean waves. A little knowledge of geology can take you far—or at least provide more of an escape from the everyday world than you might think.

Acknowledgments

Many friends contributed more than they know to this book, and without them this volume would still be in the netherworld of unborn books. John Eliot Allen's guidance gave the book direction. Joe and Marge Bernard provided long-time logistic and moral support. Ted Brown provided expertise from the hiker's perspective. Many geologists, especially Bev Vogt, Tracy Vallier, Ted Fremd, Mark Ferns, and Terry Geisler, contributed expertise. My energetic Alaskan Malamute trail companions, Wolf and Bear, insisted that I get the hikes done. Most important, my husband David's patience, encouragement, understanding, advice, support, and proofreading prowess brought this book from the shadows of an idea into the sunlight of reality. However, I take all responsibility for any errors or omissions of geologic facts, dates, or other information.

—*Ellen Morris Bishop*

Introduction

Although the dimensions and timescale of geology often seem remote from human experience, in fact we satisfy our every need from the earth. The air we breathe came first as gases from a cooling planet, and is renewed each day by plants that depend on soils crafted from rocks. All our metals, concrete, plastics, fuels, and even wood and food supply come directly or indirectly from stone. Geology controls our water supplies. Groundwater follows some rock formations and is absent from others, is trapped in faults, and is funneled by joints. Rivers, creeks, and streams—and the ecosystems that depend upon them—all follow the dictates of tectonics and rocks. To live well and wisely, we need geology.

Landscapes and the geology that supports them nourish our aesthetic and spiritual needs as well as providing our physical requirements. Artists of all traditions have found inspiration in landscapes. In truth, the earth moves and breathes, although generally at timescales—both very fast and very slow—at the bounds of human understanding. Knowing how the scenery formed—whether you are photographing a volcano or a fault-bounded peak—provides new options for artistic expression. That cloud above Mount Hood may lend ominous meaning in one photograph, while in another at Steens Mountain, such a cloud may be just another suspended collection of condensed water vapor. The linearity of Steens' steep east face gains new meaning, though, if you visualize a vast rent through the earth's tender crust. So whether we are prospecting for a gold deposit, fishing for steelhead trout, or simply out for fresh air and sunshine, there is some aspect of geology that is important to each of us—whether we know it or not.

The hikes in this book lead to some of the most significant geological sites—and most spectacular scenery—in Oregon. Along the way, the text may help unravel the aspects of geology we find most interesting and relevant to our lives: How old *is* Mount Hood? How do gold deposits form? What kind of rock is that reddish stuff at Vulcan Lake? Is Spencers Butte a volcano? These hikes will teach us to ask more informed questions—and develop a deepened understanding—about the landscape and the life that dwells here.

Ancient river cobbles near Sand Pass in the Wallowa Mountains

LOOKING AT LANDSCAPES

Most of us consider geology to be the science of rocks, minerals and complicated terms. Certainly, identifying rocks and minerals is fundamental to geology. But there is more to geology than naming a rock. In a larger sense, this science seeks to understand how the earth works, and how a landscape evolved. We need to know about the processes that form and deform rocks, and about forces that we cannot hold in our hand. These include folds and faults, volcanos, and plate tectonics. To understand geology we need to examine the earth on three scales: the rock you can hold in your hand, the outcrop where you stop for lunch, and the entire mountain you plan to climb. Let's begin with small-scale geology and then look at larger topics.

MINERALS AND ROCKS

Rocks are composed of minerals, rather like a fruitcake's mixture of cherries and raisins and bits of orange peel. The vast majority of rocks are composed of fewer than seven minerals. Six of these are *silicate* minerals that contain silicon dioxide. Of these top six silicate minerals, *feldspar* and *quartz* are the most abundant rock-forming minerals. They compose most *granites* and most *sandstones.* The other silicates (*olivine, pyroxene, amphibole,* and *biotite*) are dark minerals that bear iron and magnesium, and are most notable as the black specks in granite or other igneous rocks. The seventh common rock-forming mineral, *calcite,* is a *carbonate,* specifically calcium carbonate (the major ingredient in many antacid tablets). This is the only major mineral that is soft and easily soluble in faintly acid natural groundwater. It is resistant and stable in arid climates, but dissolves readily in more humid climates.

Rocks are subdivided into three genetic categories: *igneous* (cooled from lava), *sedimentary* (deposited by water or wind), and *metamorphic* (changed from one of the other two categories by heat and/or pressure).

Igneous Rocks

Most rocks in Oregon are igneous (a Greek word meaning "fire-formed"). Except for the Klamath Mountains, where most rocks are metamorphic, or on the coast, where most, except headlands and mountaintops, are sedimentary, your safest bet in Oregon is to claim you are standing on an igneous rock.

Igneous rocks are perhaps the earth's most fundamental. Igneous rocks are formed when a molten material (such as *lava* or *magma*) cools and solidifies. Most result from the melting of the earth's *mantle.* There are two broad categories of igneous rock:

Volcanic (or extrusive) rocks—the most abundant types of igneous rock in Oregon—erupt and flow along the surface as molten lava. They solidify quickly with little time for crystals to grow, are usually fine-grained, and may also display small holes, or *vesicles* where gas bubbles collected as the lava flowed and chilled.

Common volcanic rocks include dark-colored *basalt,* gray *andesite* (named after the Andes volcanos), and light-colored *rhyolite* and *dacite.*

Columbia River basalt dikes cut through granitic rocks in the Wallowa Mountains.

Basalt covers much of eastern Oregon and the Columbia River Gorge, supports coastal headlands, and provides a foundation for the High Cascades. The peaks of the High Cascades are mostly andesite. Dacite, rhyolite, and *obsidian* (a quick-chilled, glassy version of rhyolite) are very viscous and cannot flow very far. These light-colored rocks usually compose *domes*—piles of viscous lava built atop the vent—high on volcanic peaks.

Some volcanic rocks are composed of ash rather than lava. Volcanic ash that is compressed into rock is known as *tuff*. A rock called *welded tuff* forms when ash that is still hot literally sticks or welds together. These rocks erupt in torrid clouds of ash called *ignimbrites*, and can form extensive layers.

Volcanic mudflows, or *lahars*, are considered both volcanic and sedimentary in nature. Modern lahars swept down Washington's Toutle River when Mount St. Helens erupted in 1980. These hot mudflows are unleashed when the heat of an eruption melts snow and glacial ice, sending a torrent of hot water, boulders, and ash with the consistency of hot concrete rushing down a volcano's slopes.

Plutonic (or **intrusive**) **rocks** are formed if a lava never reaches the surface and cools slowly underground. *Plutonic* rocks are coarser-grained and often have a salt-and-pepper appearance. They include *gabbro*, a dark-colored equivalent of basalt; *diorite*, a lighter, often gray-colored rock which looks like granite; and *granite*, everybody's favorite, which tends to be light in color, although there are dark pink or red granites in the Colorado and Wyoming Rockies.

Most people use the term "granite" for any coarse-grained, light-colored igneous rock. But many rocks that look like granite are not really granite by geologists' definition. They do not have the right percentages of the minerals quartz and feldspar. In Oregon, most rocks that look like granite are technically *granodiorite* or *tonalite*, with less quartz than a "true" granite. The proper catch-all term for a granite look-alike is *granitic* or *granitoid* rock.

IGNEOUS ROCKS

Color Minerals	Intrusive (Plutonic)	Extrusive (Volcanic)
Light-colored Quartz, feldspar, biotite	Granite Granodiorite	Rhyolite Dacite
Gray Feldspar, hornblende	Diorite	Andesite
Dark gray or green Feldspar, pyroxene	Gabbro	Basalt
Dark green with red-brown outside Pyroxene, olivine	Peridotite	No extrusive form in Oregon

Cooled bodies of plutonic rocks may represent the solidified *magma* chambers beneath long-extinct and eroded volcanos, or may be a body of molten rock that cooled without erupting. They come in many different sizes and shapes. The largest bodies, by definition greater than 100 square kilometers in area, are known as *batholiths*. Oregon's most notable batholiths include the core of the Wallowas (Wallowa batholith), the northern end of the Elkhorns (Bald Mountain batholith), Mount Ashland (Ashland pluton), and the Grants Pass pluton west of Grants Pass. Smaller bodies of plutonic rock are known as *stocks*. The narrow conduits of magma en route to the surface that slice through rock are known as *dikes*. The red-brown stripes across the granitic rocks of the Wallowa Mountains are basalt dikes. On rare occasions dictated by the right tectonic circumstances, fragments of the earth's mantle arrive on mountaintops. In Oregon, mantle rocks, known as *peridotite,* are found in the Klamath Mountains (near Vulcan Peak) and in the Blue Mountains, on the north side of Canyon Mountain.

Sedimentary Rocks

The earth's history is archived in the layers of sedimentary rocks. These rocks are formed when silt, clay, sand, or other materials are deposited

Cross-bedded sand at Yaquina head

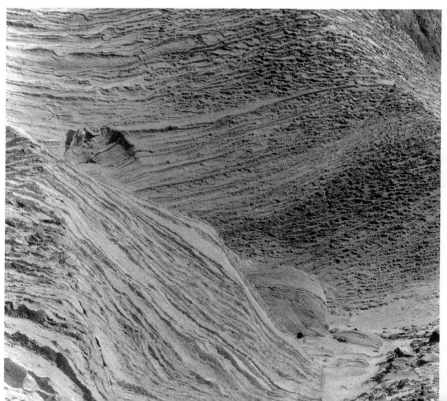

Sandstones and shales alternate in the Flournoy Formation, Marys Peak.

by water or wind; they most commonly display parallel layering (*bedding*, to geologists). Their fossils reveal primeval ecosystems, their textures evoke ancient seas. The most common Oregon sedimentary rocks are *sandstones* and *shales*. Coarse *conglomerate*, composed of sand, pebbles, and cobbles, is the trademark of an ancient river or beach. Very fine-grained sediments like shale and *chert* (a fine-grained, silica-rich sedimentary rock) indicate deep or very calm water. *Limestone* is a sedimentary rock associated with warm water and coral reefs.

Fossils are usually the only guide to the age of sedimentary rocks. In

17

fine-grained rocks, microscopic fossils of one-celled plants or animals often provide clues to the age of the ancient seafloor. Fossils also help us understand how far dispersed the earth's plates have become: fossils of an Asiatic sea cap the Elkhorn Mountains; corals crown the summits of the Wallowas.

SEDIMENTARY ROCKS

Particle Size	Rock Name
Pebbles and cobbles	Conglomerate
Sand	Sandstone
Silt and clay	Shale
Silica-rich ooze	Chert
Calcium-carbonate ooze or extremely fine-grained precipitation; coral reef	Limestone

Examining a plant fossil from the John Day Formation

Metamorphic Rocks

Metamorphic rocks are merely igneous or sedimentary rocks that have been changed by heat and pressure. In Oregon, there are basically just four kinds of metamorphic rock: *greenstone, marble, schist,* and *amphibolite.* The textures and colors vary from rock to rock, but the names and mineralogy are the same. The metamorphic changes in heat and pressure vary from the barely discernible metamorphism of the sediments in the Wallowa or Aldrich Mountains to the extremely high-pressure metamorphism that changed seabed shales into *blueschist* near Mitchell and at Condrey Mountain in the Klamaths.

Greenstone—a catch-all term for gently metamorphosed basalt or other igneous rock—is the most abundant metamorphic rock in Oregon. It is green because iron-bearing minerals in the original rock alter to green minerals during metamorphism. Greenstones abound in Hells Canyon and along the Rogue River. A related rock, *serpentinite,* occurs in the Klamath Mountains.

Marble is heated and recrystallized limestone. Marbles can be hard, resistant rocks. Or they may be crumbly and difficult to climb, like some marbles in the Wallowa Mountains that have developed large calcite crystals and a texture like coarsely granulated sugar.

Coarse feldspar preserved in the greenstone of Hells Canyon

Schist is a fragile rock. This flaky, or *friable,* rock develops thin layers of mica and other shiny minerals. Schist is very rare in Oregon, found only in a few locations in the Blue and Klamath Mountains.

Amphibolite is a dark, banded rock that often exhibits small folds or flaky layers. It develops where very high temperature and pressure have affected rocks. It is even more rare than schist in Oregon.

Joints in sandstone

A small fault offsets the bedding in these sedimentary rocks near Mitchell.

FOLDS, FAULTS, AND STRUCTURAL GEOLOGY

The earth is neither a stable nor a gentle place. Continents collide. Sea-floors spread. Mountains rise. Volcanos erupt. All this activity stresses rocks. In people, stress produces wrinkles and gray hair. In rocks, it produces folds, faults, and cracks.

While geologists classify different types of folds, the only thing the hiker need recognize is that *folds*—any type of fold at any scale—result from compression sometime in the rock's history. The broad, open folds in Columbia River basalt west of The Dalles, the crinkled chert at Rainbow Rock just north of Brookings, or the microscopic crenulations in the minerals of the Josephine peridotite at Vulcan Lake all mean the same thing: the rocks were subjected to stress, and folded or wrinkled as a result.

Faults are physical breaks in the rock where one portion of the earth's crust has moved past another. Like folds, they occur at all scales. Some faults develop where rock is pushed together and is too brittle to bend. Others develop where rocks are extended or pulled apart. All faults show *offset*—the displacement of one side relative to another. Motion along faults

21

Joints in granodiorite, Elkhorn Mountains

may be measured in millimeters, or in hundreds of miles. *Joints* are cracks or separations along which there has been no movement.

OREGON AND PLATE TECTONICS

The basic tenet of plate tectonics is that the earth's crust is composed of plates of low-density continental rocks (granites) and heavier oceanic crust (basalt) that move across the earth's surface. The motion is driven by convection currents in the earth's mantle—hot, dense material composed of the rock peridotite.

North America's westward motion was driven by the opening of the Atlantic Ocean—or *seafloor spreading*—that began 200 million years ago and continues today. The seafloor on which the continent rides is pushed and pulled back down into the mantle (rather like a huge conveyor belt). The process is called *subduction*, and the zone where the seafloor plunges back down into the mantle is called a *subduction zone*. Volcanos usually develop above the subduction zone, and it is these volcanic islands that North America collided with to create Oregon's first land in the Klamaths and Blue Mountains.

The islands and scraps of seafloor that were added to the continent are called *terranes*, or sometimes *exotic terranes*. A terrane can be defined informally as a group of rocks produced by unique geologic processes in one location and transported to a new location by plate tectonics. The terranes of the Blue Mountains are an example. Each terrane represents a different part of a complex island arc system—the volcanos, the subduction zone, etc.—that collided with the adjacent continent. Sometimes, as in the Klamaths, the island arcs also collide with one another, producing a welter of terranes that are then added to the continent in one package. Western North America has long been a sort of terrane station, where the continent grows westward a little farther as each terrane arrives.

Other plate tectonic forces have contributed to Oregon's history as well. These include the clockwise rotation of the Klamath Mountains, Coast Range, and Cascades westward. During the last 20 million years, this linear band of tectonic blocks has swung westward like a pendulum with its pivot point just north of Longview, Washington. This rotational motion may be linked to the expansion of the Basin and Range in southeast Oregon, and to the faults of the Olympic–Wallowa lineament fault in northeast Oregon.

There are undoubtedly other forces, as yet unrecognized, at work sculpting Oregon and our planet. After all, in 1965, plate tectonics was still the controversial hypothesis of a few graduate students, and tectonic rotation was not even dreamed of. As long as we continue to observe the earth, we will see new things and make fresh discoveries. Which is why, after all, we go hiking in the first place.

OREGON'S GEOLOGIC PROVINCES

Ask when Oregon began and you will get many answers: in 1804 with the arrival of Lewis and Clark; in 1792 when Captain Gray sailed up the Columbia River; 10,000 years ago when the first Native Americans settled along the coast and Columbia River. But for the geologist, Oregon's history begins dimly 400 million years ago, in warm seas off the coast of Idaho where volcanic islands erupted and coral reefs prospered.

Oregon has built westward ever since, sweeping up volcanic islands and scraps of seafloor onto its shores as North America moved westward. First the continent added the island systems that form the Blue Mountains and the Klamaths. In the ensuing 40 million years, volcanic eruptions welded these new pieces to North America, building the shore gradually from Mitchell in central Oregon to the western slopes of the Cascades. The Coast Range began as *seamounts* (a series of submarine volcanos), then was scraped from the seafloor by North America's relentless western migration and added to the continent 20 million years ago. The new coastline lay about where ocean waves break today. In these last 20 million years, basalts surged across Oregon, the High Cascade peaks appeared, and the greatest floods known on the planet swept down the Columbia River system and out to sea.

Oregon's geology parallels its geography. Each set of rocks defines a different landscape, a unique climate, and different challenges for the hiker. From oldest to youngest, Oregon's major geologic subdivisions are:

The Klamath Mountains—Mostly rocks of the seafloor and tropical volcanic archipelagos, 300 to 100 million years in age, the Klamaths were added to North America about 100 million years ago.

The Blue Mountains—Though similar to the Klamath Mountains, the

The way cars are stacked in this wrecking yard resembles the way terranes are stacked in the Klamaths and Blue Mountains.

Blue Mountains generally represent a single island system, 300 to 190 million years in age, which was added to North America about 100 million years ago. These old seafloor rocks are covered by younger volcanic rocks, including the Columbia River basalts.

The Cascades—The Cascades are two mountains ranges in one. Both are volcanic. The Western Cascades, 40 to about 10 million years in age, occupy the Cascade foothills; the High Cascades, whose reigning volcanos are less than 1 million years old, parade as scenic peaks.

The Coast Range—These low mountains are composed of seafloor sediments and seamounts. Their rocks are 45 to 25 million years old, but were added to North America only 20 million years ago.

The Willamette Valley—North of the Klamath Mountains, between the Coast Range and the Cascades, lies the Willamette Valley. Geologists used to think this valley simply lay passively between two mountain ranges. But we are discovering that the Willamette Valley is a dynamic place. During the last 10 million years earthquakes have sculpted this landscape. The Portland Basin, which lies at the northern end of the Willamette Valley, is among the most seismically active areas in Oregon.

The Columbia River Gorge—Most closely allied with the Cascades, the Gorge is lined with basalts of the Columbia River group from 15 to 6 million years in age. These basalts erupted from vents in eastern Oregon and Washington. Some followed the ancestral channel of the Columbia all the way to the sea.

The Basin and Range—This vast region of southeast Oregon is seismically active. Here, the earth's crust is stretching, and has been for the last 15 million years. Volcanic rocks predominate; a few layered sedimentary rocks represent accumulations of ash in shallow lakes. The basalt rimrocks of Abert Rim, Poker Jim Rim, and Steens Mountain are about 16 million years in age.

The Owyhees—Lying unobtrusively east of the Basin and Range, the Owyhees are a dissected upland of giant volcanic *calderas* and fine-grained gold deposits. The huge volcanos erupted 15 to 10 million years ago. A few young basalts, less than 1 million years in age, have flooded local basins and created rubbly rims.

The Deschutes Basin—Between Bend and Warm Springs, and near The Dalles, ash, stream sediments, and lavas from the Cascades accumulated between 7 and 4 million years ago. Today they form a volcanic layer cake of ash-rich sediments and volcanic flows that comprises the Deschutes Basin.

The High Lava Plains—A chain of volcanos, mostly rhyolite and basalt eruptions, the High Lava Plains become progressively younger to the west.

The most recent eruptions built Newberry Volcano. Here the Big Obsidian Flow, a glassy rhyolite flow, is only 1,300 years in age and among Oregon's youngest volcanic rocks.

GEARING UP FOR FIELD GEOLOGY

Field geologists are merely hikers with some extra knowledge of the earth sciences and a specific problem to solve. By using this book and learning a few basics, you can become a field geologist, too.

WHAT TO BRING

Begin with the basics for hiking, including comfortable and appropriate clothes, sturdy boots, a day pack or backpack, a hat, sunscreen, a whistle, a space blanket, et cetera. Be sure to always carry the Ten Essentials: extra clothing, extra food and water, sunglasses, pocket knife, candle or firestarter, flashlight with extra bulb and batteries, first-aid kit, waterproof matches, compass, and map. Use topographic maps, preferably 7.5' USGS maps, and if a published geologic map of the area is available, you might find it helpful. For more information on maps, see the next section, Books and Maps.

To explore and understand geologic features, a few other items to include are a hand lens, preferably 10x, to examine the small-scale features of rocks; a hammer, to break open rocks so you can examine a fresh surface (weathered surfaces often do not even remotely resemble the real rock); and safety glasses. It is *critical* to wear eye protection, and to keep others at a safe distance when breaking rock with a hammer (or with anything else), because rock chips and steel slivers from the hammer frequently fly in all directions, and can seriously injure eyes or cut you or bystanders. Bring safety glasses and use them.

A notebook is handy to record observations. Commercially available field notebooks are more durable than spiral-bound books from stationery stores, but any notebook is better than none. If you wish to collect samples, consider taking something to wrap them in so that they are protected and your gear is protected from your samples. Newspaper is light, cheap, and effective. A felt-tip, waterproof pen can be useful to mark sample numbers on each rock and key it to notes about where it was collected or other thoughts.

The two most essential things to take are focused curiosity and keen observation. These are inexpensive, lightweight, and indispensable. And everyone has access to them.

Using a hand lens for a geologist's-eye view of a rock

BOOKS AND MAPS

Because this book is not meant as a comprehensive field guide to solving all geologic problems, you might wish to invest in a book or two specifically about field geology. See Recommended Reading at the end of this book for some suggestions. Many technical papers that explain geology in great detail are also available in larger libraries.

Topographic maps provide information about elevation and topography as well as trail location. The standard, and most easily readable, is the US Geological Survey's 7.5' quadrangle map format. Other USGS maps, including USGS 1:100,000 scale, are available as well.

Topographic maps of most wilderness areas are published by or in co-operation with the US Forest Service and Bureau of Land Management, and may be obtained at most ranger districts or in outdoor stores.

Geologic maps show the type of rock formations present. Most have a topographic base, so they provide both geologic and topographic information. However, the topographic information may be difficult to read, so a separate topographic map is recommended. A list of geologic maps for the hikes in this book is found in Appendix A, Geologic Maps.

Geologic maps and USGS topographic maps, as well as many other books and some geologic and topographic maps, are available from The Nature of Oregon, a sales office of the Oregon Department of Geology and Mineral Industries and US Forest Service, located in the State Office Building in northeast Portland.

For addresses of these agencies and other resources, see Appendix B, Addresses.

HOW TO USE THIS BOOK

Each chapter is devoted to one of Oregon's ten geologic provinces; the chapters follow a geographic progression from west to east. Each chapter begins with an overview of the geologic province, then lists one or more hikes in the area.

Each hike is numbered, and its title, subtitle, and summary provide information on location and special features to help you quickly select hikes that interest you. An information block further summarizes the hike's profile:

Distance: The hike's length is given in miles, round trip unless stated otherwise.

Elevation: The change in elevation is given by listing the hike's low and high points in feet.

Difficulty: Ratings are easy, moderate, or strenuous. Easy hikes are on level terrain, are usually less than 2 miles long, and follow well-marked, broad, unobstructed trails. Strenuous hikes traverse more than 2,000 feet in elevation change, follow rugged trails, and/or require either long day hikes of more than 8 miles or an overnight pack trip. Moderate hikes fall in between these two extremes.

Topographic maps: The USGS 7.5' quadrangle map(s) for the hike is listed.

Geologic maps: Geologic maps in Appendix A, Geologic Maps have been given a unique number; here, the map(s) for the hike is indicated by that number. Refer to the appendix for the map's name and facts of publication.

OREGON'S GEOLOGIC TIMETABLE

Twenty significant events that shaped Oregon's landscape

Millions of years ago	Geologic era	Geologic event
0.0002 (the year 1790)	Holocene	Most recent major eruptions of Mount Hood
0.0004 (the year 1600)	Holocene	Bridge of the Gods landslide dams the Columbia
0.0012 (1,200 years ago)	Holocene	Eruptions of Rock Mesa at South Sister and Big Obsidian Flow, Newberry Volcano
0.007 (6,800 years ago)	Holocene	Cataclysmic eruption of Mount Mazama (Crater Lake)
0.012–0.015 (12,000–15,000 years ago)	Pleistocene	Missoula (Bretz) floods repeatedly scour Columbia Gorge and flood the Hermiston basin and Willamette Valley
0.73 (730,000 years ago)	Pleistocene	Mount Hood and other High Cascade peaks first erupt, continuing to build during Pleistocene glaciation
2–3	Pliocene	Snake River begins cutting Hells Canyon
11	Miocene	Faulting on Olympic–Wallowa lineament begins uplifting the Wallowa Mountains
14–18	Miocene	Most Columbia River basalts erupt, covering much of eastern Oregon and Washington and part of western Idaho; eruption of major Owyhee calderas (15–16); eruption of Steens and other Basin and Range basalt (16)
20–25	Oligocene	Oregon Coast Range is added to the continent
29–35	Oligocene	John Day Formation (Painted Hills) erupted from local vents and as windblown ash from active Western Cascades; coast is on west edge of Cascades; temperate climate
40–50	Eocene	Clarno volcanos active in central Oregon; subtropic climate; Tyee sandstones deposited; seamounts that will form the Coast Range erupt; Eohippus in central Oregon
90–110	Cretaceous	Blue Mountain island arc becomes part of North America
120	Cretaceous	Klamath Mountains island arc block becomes part of North America
130	Cretaceous	Diverse islands of Klamaths collect into single "Klamath" block
120–160	Jurassic to Cretaceous	Granitic magmas intrude the Klamaths and Blue Mountains island arc terranes begin collision with North America
130–160	Jurassic	Volcanic systems of Western Klamath terrane (Dry Butte terrane and peridotites near Vulcan Peak/ Vulcan Lake) active; in Blue Mountains, oceanic sediments cover extinct island arc volcanos
165	Jurassic	Volcanos of Snow Camp terrane and sheeted dikes along Rogue River active in Klamath island arc system; sedimentary rocks include plant fossils similar to contemporary Coon Hollow Formation in Hells Canyon
225–235	Triassic	Younger generation of volcanos in the Blue Mountains island arc erupts on islands in the Pacific; sedimentary rocks of the Wallowa Mountains deposited; in Klamaths, limestones of Applegate Group (Oregon Caves) deposited
275	Permian	First generation of volcanos in Blue Mountains island arc; coral reefs flourish around island volcanos

Note: This timetable provides a few significant events in Oregon's geologic past. It is not meant as a comprehensive list.

Precautions: Crucial information regarding access, trail conditions, and safety concerns are listed here.

For information: The agency that manages the land in which the hike is located is given here; addresses are found in Appendix B, Addresses.

Following the information block is *About the Landscape,* which highlights the geologic features of interest on the hike. Last is the *Trail Guide,* which describes how to get to the trailhead and gives details about the hike's route.

At the back of the book are a Glossary of geologic terms, a Geologic Time Chart, and a list of Recommended Reading.

THE CHANGING LANDSCAPE

When we enter the backcountry we step away from processes that humans control and into the changing landscape. Here, what seem like catastrophes to us—floods, forest fires, earthquakes, windstorms, and volcanic eruptions— are merely planetary housecleaning. No place on earth is immune to catastrophic change, and the trails discussed in this book are no exception. For example, in 1995, high winds felled trees and closed trails on Marys Peak while floods and landslides damaged trails in the Columbia River Gorge. In 1996, major forest fires swept through Hells Canyon, the Elkhorn Mountains, the Strawberry Mountains, and Smith Rock State Park.

Hikers especially need to be aware of this fact and check trail conditions with the pertinent agency before embarking on a lengthy trip. Remember, too, that the U. S. Forest Service's policy of returning fire to the ecosystem means that lightning-caused forest fires, especially in wilderness areas, are often allowed to burn. Be aware of forest conditions and storm activity when hiking in late summer. And as you hike, consider how past catastrophes have created the landscape that you, for the moment, are a part of.

A NOTE ABOUT SAFETY

Safety is an important concern in all outdoor activities. No guidebook can alert you to every hazard or anticipate the limitations of every reader. Therefore, the information presented and the techniques described in this book are not representations that a particular activity will be safe for you or your party. When you engage in any of the activities described in this book, you assume responsibility for your own safety. Under normal conditions, such excursions require the usual attention to traffic, road and trail conditions, weather, terrain, the capabilities of your party, and other factors. Keeping informed on current conditions and exercising common sense are the keys to a safe, enjoyable outing.

The Mountaineers

Chapter 1.
THE KLAMATH MOUNTAINS

Sedimentary rocks near Illahe

The Klamath Mountains are the oldest and most eclectic range in Oregon. They spill over into California and encompass the welter of peaks called the Siskiyous. Their rocks include slivers of the earth's mantle, seafloor, and old volcanos; scraps of the continent; and gold-bearing granites. Their exotic geology is similar to that of the Blue Mountains: they once were islands far from the Oregon coast, and were added to North America more than 100 million years ago.

But unlike the terranes of the Blue Mountains that represent different parts of the same island arc, the terranes of the Klamaths have been shorn from a multitude of arcs. By hiking from one part of the Klamath Mountains to another, you can visit islands that were formed millions of years and hundreds of miles apart. Generally, the rocks and terranes of the Klamaths are older the farther inland you go. The principal terranes of the Klamath Mountains that are recognized by geologists include:

The Sixes River terrane includes scraps of Cretaceous seamounts and ocean floor found near Cape Blanco.

ISLAND ARCS, SUBDUCTION ZONES, AND EXOTIC TERRANES

The tranquillity of many South Sea islands is a calm veneer above geologic turmoil. For these islands, as well as chains like the Aleutians, Kuriles, and the Japanese archipelago, mark places where the seafloor plunges 430 miles into the earth's mantle, down an oceanic trench, spawning volcanos and earthquakes on the plate above. On a map these chains of islands above the oceanic trench or subduction zone often present a curving arc. Thus, they are called an *island arc*. Volcanos that develop on a continent above a subduction zone, like the Cascades or the Andes, are called a volcanic arc.

Island arcs are often swept up and added to the prow of continents. As plate tectonics moves a continent, the seafloor in front of the large landmass usually descends down a subduction zone. Eventually the continent reaches the subduction zone, and collides with the island arc above it. In this collision, the island arc is added or accreted to the continent, and eventually becomes the newest land. The old arc—now the newest part of a continent's leading edge—is called a *terrane*.

Western North America has grown westward more than 800 miles

Snow Camp terrane represents the magma chambers beneath Cretaceous island arc volcanos. It is exposed on the lower Rogue River (hike 5, Wild Rogue River).

Gold Beach terrane is a zone of Jurassic sedimentary and igneous rocks found today along the Oregon coast between Gold Beach and Cape Blanco.

Yolla Bolly terrane incorporates the sandstones and shales of a Jurassic beach. These rocks extend from Brookings northward.

Western Klamath terrane is an extensive Jurassic island arc complex. The five recognized *subterranes*, or subdivisions of the main terrane, represent parts of the island arc. They include the Rogue River subterrane—arc volcanos—and the Dry Butte subterrane—the roots of those volcanos. Hike 3, Vulcan Lakes, traverses these rocks.

Applegate or **Western Paleozoic and Triassic terrane** represents the oldest rocks of Oregon's Klamath Mountains and includes fragments of ancient ocean crust. The marbles of Oregon Caves (hike 2) and the rocks of Red Butte on hike 4, Pacific Crest Trail, are part of this terrane.

from its core in the last 600,000 years by this process of accretion. The Appalachians, from Newfoundland to South Carolina, were adopted in a similar manner.

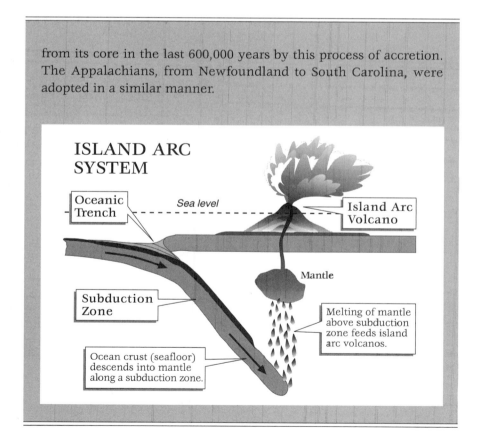

ISLAND ARC SYSTEM

Oceanic Trench

Sea level

Island Arc Volcano

Mantle

Subduction Zone

Melting of mantle above subduction zone feeds island arc volcanos.

Ocean crust (seafloor) descends into mantle along a subduction zone.

Many of these terranes collided with one another to form a collage of terranes before they encountered North America. By the time the continent arrived, many had amalgamated into a mini-continent. The Klamath terranes became part of North America by about 100 million years ago. Lava flows from the Cascades covered the Klamath terranes' connection with the continent; sedimentary rocks of the Coast Range buried the old rocks on the north.

Hike 1

UPPER TABLE ROCK

ANCESTRAL CHANNEL OF THE ROGUE RIVER

An easy walk up to an ancient riverbed provides an exceptional view of the modern Rogue River and the Rogue valley.

DISTANCE ■ 1.5–2 miles one way

ELEVATION ■ 1,300 to 2,050 feet

DIFFICULTY ■ Easy

TOPOGRAPHIC MAP ■ Sam's Valley

GEOLOGIC MAP ■ 2

PRECAUTIONS ■ Avoid contact with and transporting flowers or seeds of yellowstar thistle, an exotic pest plant that prospers on Table Rocks. Take adequate water; there is no potable water on Table Rocks.

FOR INFORMATION ■ Medford Bureau of Land Management office

About the Landscape: The large, flat-topped mesas north of Medford (called, rather dully, Upper Table Rock and Lower Table Rock) overlie the Klamath terranes. They look large and square, but a map view or a hiker's exploration prove them to be horseshoe-shaped. Table Rocks preserve the form of the ancestral Rogue River's meanders. They are a classic example of *inverted topography*: the lowest feature—the Rogue River's ancestral channel—has now become the highest.

Near today's town of Prospect, lava from the Cascades erupted about 7 million years ago and filled the ancient river canyon with hard, resistant andesite. As time passed, the rock on either side of the lava-filled canyon eroded away, preserving the lava cast of the ancestral Rogue's course. Today, Upper and Lower Table Rocks' horseshoe-shaped forms are the remnants of that thick, canyon-filling lava flow—meanders of the ancient Rogue frozen in stone. The proximity of the modern Rogue River to this old canyon suggests that the river course and drainage patterns have changed little during the past 10 million years.

The dark volcanic rocks that cap both Upper and Lower Table Rock look like basalt. They have columns like basalt. And most references discuss the "basalt" of Table Rocks. But, technically, this rock, like many other rocks of the Cascades, is andesite. Sandstone, shale, and conglomerates lie buried beneath the 200-foot-thick volcanic flow. These sedimentary rocks, poorly exposed along the Table Rocks trails, are relicts of an even older river system, about 38 million years in age (Eocene).

Trail Guide: This hike threads through moss-festooned, gall-infested scrub oak to the base of the high andesite caprock of Upper Table Rock. This area was logged in the 1950s, and pine has not regenerated well on the dry, hot slopes.

To reach Upper Table Rock trailhead from Medford, take Table Rock Road north 5 miles. At a y intersection, turn right on Modoc Road and follow the road about 1.5 miles to the trailhead.

The trail departs the parking area and clambers up the gradual slopes of old slumps, landslides, and talus. There is little geology to see at Upper

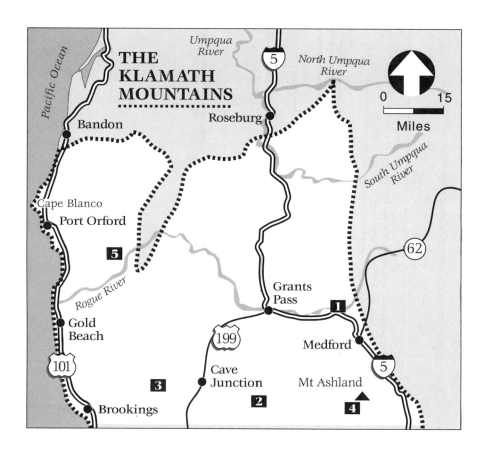

Thin soils and thick bedrock support the sparse plant life on Upper Table Rock.

Table Rock until you reach the base of the cliffs about 1 mile into the walk. Here, blocks from the adjacent cliffs form a jumbled, coarse talus. The base of the flow is buried in crumbled rocks. Once you reach the flat summit of Upper Table Rock in about 1.5 miles, the subtle geology unveils itself slowly. Elongate furrows and narrow rock crevasses define extensive vertical cracks in the lava flow. These cracks form as erosion strips away the support for the cliffs.

From where the trail emerges onto the top of Upper Table Rock, a cross-country walk 0.5 mile west reveals the opposite side's cliffs, with not only cracks but a mounded topography. Similar mounds of soils perch atop basalt bedrock worldwide. Known generally as *biscuit scabland,* they form by a variety of mechanisms. These include freezing and thawing, the activity of gophers, collection of fine material into regularly spaced mounds by violent shaking during earthquakes, and the capacity of grass and other vegetation to catch and hold windblown silts and clays. On Upper Table Rock, the mounds' north–south orientation parallels the prevailing winds and suggests that here wind was a factor in their formation.

Explore the top of Upper Table Rock, watching for the deep vertical tension cracks that cross this plateau. The overall horseshoe shape of Upper Table Rock is evident from the vantage point of its western cliffs. Return along the same route down the cliffs and along the trail to the trailhead.

Hike 2

OREGON CAVES

INSIDE A TROPICAL REEF

This guided tour of Oregon Caves National Monument is entirely underground.

DISTANCE ■ 1 mile

ELEVATION ■ 1,200 to 2,000 feet

DIFFICULTY ■ Moderate

TOPOGRAPHIC MAP ■ Oregon Caves

GEOLOGIC MAPS ■ 1, 5, 6

PRECAUTIONS ■ The National Park Service-sponsored 90-minute commercial tour (admission fee $7.50 in 1995) requires climbing 210 vertical feet on skinny, slippery metal staircases.

FOR INFORMATION ■ Oregon Caves National Monument

About the Landscape: The marble of Oregon Caves National Monument is part of the Applegate terrane, a coral reef that flourished in tropical seas. These rocks are similar in age and origin to the Martin Bridge limestone of the Wallowa Mountains, leading some geologists to hypothesize a connection between the two.

The marble of Oregon Caves formed about 200 million years ago (Triassic) as a limestone coral reef in the Pacific Ocean far south and west of where Oregon is today. As sediments piled up on the seafloor, the limestones were buried slowly beneath a thick pile of shales. Deep burial, plus the force of collision with North America, recrystallized the limestone and transformed it into a low grade of marble.

Granitic *plutons* intruded the marble of Oregon Caves and the Applegate terrane 160 million years ago, about the time these Klamath Mountain rocks collided with North America. They became part of North America more than 100 million years ago. Since that time, the rocks that form Oregon Caves have been folded, tilted, and faulted. All this activity created faults and cracks in the rock. Oregon Caves were formed as these imperfections were gradually enlarged through the dissolving and eroding action mostly of groundwaters, rather than of surface streams. However, significant erosion and deposition of silt and gravels into Oregon Caves was accomplished by rivers or streams that flowed into sinkholes and then deposited their gravels in the passageways below.

Trail Guide: The guided hike filters through several narrow passages before entering a chamber where guides explain the processes of cave formation, the types of rock that caves develop in, and the differences between

Stalactites and stalagmites in Oregon Caves (Photo courtesy Oregon Dept. of Transportation)

caverns in limestone and caverns developed in marble, like Oregon Caves.

From Cave Junction, drive east on Highway 46 for 19.3 miles to Oregon Caves National Monument. The tour begins at the cave entrance.

At a lights-out stop, the guide spins the tale of the cave's discovery. Other stops discuss the effects of faults and earthquakes on the cave, the growth of stalactites and stalagmites and other cave-related rock formations, and the biology and life cycles of the cave's bats. Several stops examine the fanciful dripstone and flowstone formations that attract people to caves. And you can see the actual pencil signature of pioneering geologist Thomas Condon, who, with his entire University of Oregon geology class, visited the cave in 1883 shortly after its discovery.

The observant hiker will find much on the tour that is not mentioned by the guide, including diorite dikes, small faults, and a variety of shale and sandstone interbedded with the cave's marble.

VULCAN LAKES

Hike 3

A Trip Across Terranes

Cross two major terranes of the Klamath Mountains and see unusual carnivorous plants.

DISTANCE ■ **8 miles**

ELEVATION ■ **3,200 to 4,000 feet**

DIFFICULTY ■ Moderate

TOPOGRAPHIC MAP ■ Vulcan Peak

GEOLOGIC MAPS ■ 3, 4

PRECAUTIONS ■ Although the drive to the trailhead is only about 36 miles, most of this is on remote gravel and dirt roads; a full gas tank is a good idea when you start. The mine shaft at the Gardiner Mine is inviting but unsafe; do not enter this mine.

FOR INFORMATION ■ Chetco Ranger District

About the Landscape: The Vulcan Peak and Chetco Peak areas once formed the base of an island arc. The red rocks of Vulcan Peak are peridotite, a rare rock that comes only from the earth's mantle. Two varieties of peridotite occur around Vulcan Peak. One has a knobby surface and is called *harzburgite*, named for similar rocks in the Harz Mountains of Germany. The other is a smooth-surfaced, tawny or red-brown rock called *dunite*, named for its dun color and for Dun Mountain, New Zealand, which is composed of similar rock.

If you examine the smooth-surfaced dunite carefully, you can find small, shiny specks about the size of coarsely ground pepper. This black mineral is chromite. In sufficient concentration it becomes an economically valuable deposit, and the rock is mined as chrome ore. Before the Kalmiopsis was a designated wilderness, a major chrome mine (the Gardiner Mine) operated here. Whereas granite is usually associated with gold, peridotite bears chrome and platinum as well as other rare metals.

North of Vulcan Lake, a major fault forms the boundary between two subterranes: the Smith River subterrane (peridotite) and the Dry Butte subterrane (gabbro). Both are part of the Western Klamath terrane—a fragment of Jurassic mantle, seafloor, and island arc volcanos. This fault is marked by layered igneous rocks and amphibolite metamorphic rocks.

Between Dry Butte and Johnson Butte, Valen Lake occupies a glacially carved cirque, nestled into the northwest side of Dry Butte. The Dry Butte–Johnson Butte Trail crosses the Valen Lake fault in the area above Valen Lake; this is the hike's final destination. The Valen Lake fault is the boundary between two major terranes of the Klamaths: the Western Klamath terrane and the Yolla Bolly terrane.

Trail Guide: This is a loop hike with spurs of varying lengths to visit Vulcan Lake, Little Vulcan Lake, and the view of Valen Lake from the Dry Butte–Johnson Butte Trail. Both Vulcan Lake and Little Vulcan Lake rest in cirques carved during the Pleistocene. Both make fine—and very popular—camping sites.

The long drive to the trailhead begins from Brookings by taking the North Bank Road up the Chetco River. At Little Redwood Campground, 10 miles from Brookings, the single-lane paved road with turnouts becomes USFS Road 1376. Pavement ends 1 mile past the campground, where the road becomes a first-rate wide gravel highway. The road crosses the Chetco River and at about 16 miles from Brookings arrives at a T intersection where a sign says KALMIOPSIS WILDERNESS, 24 MILES and points to the left. Either way will get you there, but you would do better to turn right onto USFS Road 1909 (improved greatly since the weathered sign was posted) and follow it the remaining 20 or so miles to the trailhead. At a road junction 1 mile before the Vulcan Peak trailhead, continue left to Vulcan Lakes/Peak.

Trail 110A, to Vulcan Lakes, leaves the trailhead parking area along an old road. From this broad, level entry road, the trail branches to the right and climbs over the ridge ahead toward Vulcan Lake. This path rises through red-brown peridotite—once part of the earth's mantle. A short spur trail about 0.75 mile into the walk coaxes the hiker to Vulcan Lake, less than 0.5 mile away, and its dark shoreline lined with red-brown peridotite.

From Vulcan Lake, retrace your steps to trail 110, which continues on

Layered peridotite outcrops near Little Vulcan Lake

toward Little Vulcan Lake. This trail is sometimes difficult to follow, but is well marked by hiker's cairns. To the north and 0.5 mile downslope of Vulcan Lake, another short spur leads to Little Vulcan Lake, which harbors a botanical reserve where pitcher plants prosper.

On the rise just north of Little Vulcan Lake, excellent exposures of glacially polished peridotite can be found. An exploration of the 200-yard-wide area between the lake and the abrupt drop into the valley below reveals beautiful examples of layered peridotite, as well as the rectangular pattern of joints that dictate much of the regional landscape.

From Little Vulcan Lake, retrace the spur path to trail 112A, which leads north to the Gardiner Mine and on to Dry Butte. Trail 112A is well marked by cairns. The footpath merges with an old road after about 0.5 mile, and the road continues 0.25 mile to the abandoned Gardiner Mine. You can find chunks of shiny black chrome ore in the nearby piles of mine tailings.

From the mine, the road leads another 0.25 mile to the ridge top. The layered rocks and amphibolites of the Madstone Cabin thrust fault appear along this ridge top. They have been squeezed into banded black and white rocks called amphibolite. The Madstone Cabin thrust fault has not been active for perhaps 100 million years, but it is a major fault that divides two terranes. As you proceed along the trail, you cross gradually from the Smith River subterrane (mantle peridotite) to the Dry Butte subterrane (gabbro of the ocean floor).

At the ridge top, turn right (north) along an old logging/mining road (Road 1110). The walk to the end of this road is an easy one; in 1 mile merge with the more traditional trail that continues toward Dry Butte and Johnson Butte. This trail leads into the younger gabbro on the north side of the Madstone Cabin thrust fault. Halfway between Dry Butte and Johnson Butte, just above Valen Lake, the bedrock changes abruptly from tough gabbros to soft shales.

Valen Lake is significant for a second geological reason: the Valen Lake thrust fault that cuts through the slope just above the lake. Like the Madstone Cabin fault that you crossed earlier, the Valen Lake fault has not been active since the Klamaths became part of North America. Long ago this major fault lifted the old igneous rocks of the Western Klamath terrane (which includes the peridotite and gabbro you have just hiked across) up and over the younger sedimentary shales of the Yolla Bolly terrane.

As you near Johnson Butte, you will find the intersection of trails 1110 and 1112. This means you have crossed the Valen Thrust—the mission of this hike—and can return the same way you came along trail 1110 and along the old mine access road to trails 112A and 110A to the Vulcan Peak/Vulcan Lakes trailhead.

GEOLOGIC TIMETABLE 1: THE KLAMATHS

Five significant events that shaped the landscape

Millions of years ago	Geologic era	Geologic event
7	Miocene	Basalt erupts from Cascades, fills Rogue River Canyon; erosion gradually strips away canyon walls, leaving Table Rocks as remnants of the basalt that filled the canyon
100–130	Cretaceous	Klamath terranes amalgamate, then become part of North America
140–160	Jurassic	Granitic plutons of Klamaths, including Mount Ashland and Grants Pass plutons, form
140–165	Jurassic	Volcanic systems that formed Dry Butte terrane, rocks near Vulcan Peaks/Lake (Josephine peridotite), and Snow Camp terrane along the wild Rogue River active
225–280	Permian	Western Paleozoic and Triassic belt rocks: and Triassic Limestones of Oregon Caves form; oldest volcanic systems of Oregon Klamaths

PACIFIC CREST TRAIL

MOUNT ASHLAND TO WRANGLE GAP

Visit an example of how a pluton intrudes, digests, and assimilates the surrounding country rock.

DISTANCE ■ 18 miles

ELEVATION ■ 5,800 to 6,200 feet

DIFFICULTY ■ Easy

TOPOGRAPHIC MAPS ■ Mount Ashland, Siskiyou Peak, Dutchman Peak

GEOLOGIC MAPS ■ 5, 6

PRECAUTIONS ■ Because of this hike's length, it is recommended as an overnight backpack.

FOR INFORMATION ■ Ashland Ranger District

About the Landscape: The Ashland pluton is one of eight major granitic intrusions in the Klamath Mountains. This large body of granitic rocks is mostly granodiorite, 160 to 147 million years old. It has deformed, baked, and digested the rocks of the Applegate terrane, the oldest rocks of the Oregon Klamath Mountains.

Granitic outcrops along the Pacific Crest Trail

This relatively level hike explores Mount Ashland and the Ashland pluton. One of the best parts of the journey is the exceptional lesson of how the Mount Ashland granitic pluton intruded the surrounding shale. This process is exposed in roadcuts on the way to the hike's beginning. Plan to stop and check out several of these roadcuts and perhaps arrange an auto-hiker relay if you drive up the mountain with a companion.

Trail Guide: The trail follows the Pacific Crest Trail (PCT) along the ridge crest, paralleling a major USFS road, from Grouse Gap to Big Red Mountain and Wrangle Gap.

From Interstate 5 south of Ashland, take exit 6, Mount Ashland exit, and take Mount Ashland Road toward Mount Ashland Ski Area. This road becomes USFS Road 20 at the Siskiyou National Forest boundary. High roadcuts from mile 2 to mile 4 along this paved and well-maintained roadway show, in progression, (1) sedimentary rocks cross-cut and intruded by small granitic dikes; (2) sedimentary rocks enmeshed in a network of granite; (3) dark, angular globs of recrystallized sedimentary rock (*xenoliths*) floating in a granitic matrix; (4) irregular, small blobs of recrystallized sedimentary rock entombed in granitic rock; and (5) granitic rocks with a few small, dark, rounded xenoliths.

Light-colored granitic rock intrudes dark shale along Mount Ashland Road.

Xenoliths in granodiorite, Klamath Mountains

At Grouse Gap, 1.5 miles west of the Mount Ashland Ski Area, at the intersection of USFS 20 and the PCT, also called USFS Trail 2000, find the trailhead. Parking is available at the Grouse Gap shelter if you plan to be on the trail overnight.

The first 5 miles meander through the Ashland pluton. Large outcrops are rare along the hike, but many boulders and small exposures along the trail show off the Ashland pluton's textures and rock types. Notable things to look for include the large square pink to white *orthoclase* (potassium-rich) feldspar crystals that are a hallmark of many Ashland pluton rocks, and dark, strung-out xenoliths, or relicts of the old sedimentary rocks intruded, partly melted, and captured by the pluton. These features are prominent near Grouse Gap. The closer you approach the edge of the Ashland pluton, the finer-grained the granitic rocks become. Within 200 yards of this contact, the granitic rocks develop a noticeable layering or, in geological terms, *foliation*.

At about 5 miles, the rocks change abruptly from the monotonous gray of the Ashland pluton's granodiorite to finer-grained metamorphic rocks. The trail makes a wide swing to the north around the aptly, if unimaginatively, named Big Red Mountain. It is composed of metamorphosed peridotite. Metamorphism has enhanced the reddish brown color of the weathered stone by oxidizing the iron in the peridotite. Long, bladed crystals of the magnesium-rich mineral anthophyllite form interesting textures in these rocks.

The trail eases around the barren slopes of Big Red Mountain and 1 mile farther, at Wrangle Gap, a small but shaded and well-developed campground with water and toilets waits on USFS Road 20, just beyond its intersection with the trail. You may return to the trailhead at Grouse Gap via the PCT, or walk along the USFS road for slightly different scenery.

Hike

5

WILD ROGUE RIVER

ILLAHE TO MARIAL

Explore the volcanic rocks and conduit system of an exotic island arc, plus spectacular scenery of the wild Rogue River.

DISTANCE ■ 15 miles one way

ELEVATION ■ 207 to 320 feet

DIFFICULTY ■ Moderate

TOPOGRAPHIC MAPS ■ Agness, Marial

GEOLOGIC MAPS ■ 7, 8

PRECAUTIONS ■ The hike begins at Illahe trailhead, where access does not require a 4WD vehicle, and ends at Marial, where trailhead access is on steep, narrow, and sometimes deeply muddy roads. This hike requires either a shuttle vehicle at the Marial trailhead, or an overnight at Marial before retracing the route back to the Illahe trailhead. If you plan to stay overnight at Marial Lodge, make reservations well in advance.

FOR INFORMATION ■ Siskiyou National Forest

About the Landscape: This hike tours the Snow Camp terrane, a remnant of a Jurassic island arc tossed casually into the Klamath Mountains like an anchovy onto a pizza. To the east, upstream from Marial, the older

Conglomerate outcrop along the Rogue River

Rogue River subterrane provides gold deposits. The Snow Camp terrane displays island arc crust. The rocky cliffs along the Rogue expose dikes and gabbro, but the light-colored, silica-rich volcanic rocks upstream are the upper parts of island arc volcanos. The Snow Camp terrane's rocks are an errant scrap of island arc that once looked as inviting as Bora Bora, but

47

has been changed by stress and time to the aged, wrinkled rocks that to-day confine the Rogue.

Trail Guide: Hike a portion of the upper wild and scenic Rogue River, either staying overnight at Marial and returning on the same route the next day, or leaving a shuttle vehicle at Marial before beginning the hike.

To reach the Illahe trailhead from Gold Beach, at the south end of the Highway 101 Rogue River bridge, turn east onto Jerry's Flat Road and USFS Road 33. Drive 30 miles to Curry County Road 375 (marked TO ILLAHE/ROGUE RIVER TRAIL). Illahe is 1 mile past this junction; here, cliffs and roadcuts provide an intimate view of sedimentary rocks. These are the Flournoy Formation—marine sediments about 45 million years old. Continue about 3 miles to the trailhead—an abrupt right turn into a broad field.

The first mile of the hike skirts the field and provides a good view of river terraces and the lower Rogue River. As it joins the river, the trail threads through second-growth forest. The lodge at Clay Hill, 6 miles into the hike, appears just before the Riddle Formation's brittle, thinly bedded metamorphosed shales.

One mile farther, at Tate Creek, the trail begins its journey through the magma chambers of ancient volcanos that once erupted far from Oregon's coastline. These rocks are Jurassic, dated at about 160 million years. They represent the Snow Camp terrane. At Solitude Bar, 8 miles into the hike, darker, fine-grained rocks are the metamorphosed remnants of Jurassic basalt flows. Blossom Bar rapids at 13 miles flows over ancient andesites—rocks 150 million years old that once formed a volcano like Mount Hood.

Some of the most interesting rocks of this old volcanic complex are the sheeted dikes at 14 miles that form Inspiration Point, create Stair Creek Falls, and support the last mile of trail from Inspiration Point to Marial. These sheeted dikes served as the conduits for multiple intrusions, per-haps serving as the path upward for the lavas of tens of eruptions over hundreds or thousands of years. The bands in these rocks are the chilled margins of each upward pulse of lava. The coarse-grained rocks (gabbro) enclosed by these dark, fine-grained volcanic greenstones are remnants of the solid rock these dikes cut through on their way to the surface and eruption.

At Marial, either stay overnight—camping is available, as are accommo-dations at Marial Lodge—and the next day return the way you came, or drive your shuttle vehicle back to the Illahe trailhead.

Chapter 2.
THE COAST RANGE

Chert forms craggy cliffs and stacks, Rainbow Rock near Brookings

Oregon's Coast Range perches on the northern rim of the Klamath Mountains. Like most everything else in Oregon, the Coast Range is an added attraction. It began as Eocene ocean floor sediments and seamounts and became a firm part of the continent only 20 million years ago. Pillow basalts are the foundation of the Coast Range. These lumpy basalts are well exposed on some coastal peaks and near Roseburg.

About 45 million years ago, the North American continent first began to collide with the seamounts that now crown the Coast Range. These rocks remained submerged for millions of years, creating a relatively shallow ocean basin north of the Klamath Mountains that filled with sediment. For the most part, Oregon's coast is composed of sediments draped over a skeletal structure of the seamounts' basalt.

FOLDS AND FAULTS

Rocks can respond to the forces of plate tectonics in two ways: folding and faulting. Folds (an up-fold is an *anticline;* a down-fold is a *syncline*) develop when rocks are put under compression or squeezed together. If the squeezing is rapid enough, or the rocks are brittle, then instead of folding, they are apt to break. This rupture in response to stress is called a *fault.* There are many types of faults. Each is a rock's response to a different kind of stress.

Compression produces reverse and thrust faults, where one rock is thrust up and over another. (Faults like these occur in the Klamath and Blue Mountains and in the Coast Range.) Where the earth's crust is being stretched apart, as in the Basin and Range, so-called normal faults develop, allowing rocks to separate like cold taffy being pulled apart. And where plates slip past one another on the earth's surface, the style of fault is called a *strike-slip.* In the real, three-dimensional world, most faults display a combination of these movements—both up-and-down and sideways motion at the same time. Large faults, like the San Andreas or faults on the Olympic–Wallowa Lineament (OWL) are actually a welter of smaller faults.

Faults can be recognized most easily where they offset beds of sedimentary rocks, or other horizontal strata. Because movement along the fault breaks the stone, a fault often is marked by the presence of breccia—broken, rubbly rock and clay. The bedrock surface may be polished along a fault by the pressure of one stone

The Oregon coast began to emerge from the sea 25 million years ago. By Miocene time, 18 million years ago, the coast's configuration resembled what we see today.

One of the most astounding episodes in Oregon's coastal geology occurred about 15 million years ago. At that time, there were no lofty Cascade Mountains. An ancestral Columbia River ran just south of where Mount Hood towers today. And down this ancient channel ran basalt lavas. At least twelve large flows of Columbia River basalt streamed more than 300 miles from vents in eastern Oregon and Washington all the way to Oregon's coast. The basalt headlands at Seal Rocks, Otter Rocks, Depoe Bay, Yaquina Head, Cape Kiwanda, Cape Lookout, Cape Meares, Cape Falcon, and Tillamook Head are all Columbia River basalt.

scraping against the other. This polish, and the grooves on the polished surface, are called *slickensides;* they reveal the direction of the last motion of the fault.

Rock folds

Headlands and beached logs at Cape Blanco

Oregon's coast is still forming. As the Pacific ocean floor slides beneath the shoreline, beaches on the north and south are rising. Cape Blanco is being lifted several millimeters per year—an astounding rate geologically speaking. Broad, wave-cut terraces stair-step away from the southern Oregon shore. While the north and south ends are lifting, the central Oregon Coast seems to be folding down. Hence the coastal topography around Newport and Florence is subdued and sand dunes are the landscape of tectonic choice.

About every 350 to 400 years, a major earthquake (magnitude 8 or 9) shakes the Oregon and Washington coast. The last major earthquake, as near as carbon 14 dating can determine, was in the early 1700s. In many areas along Oregon's north and south coast, a record of periodic great earthquakes is preserved in drowned marshes and in the coarse sands of *tsunami* (tidal wave) deposits.

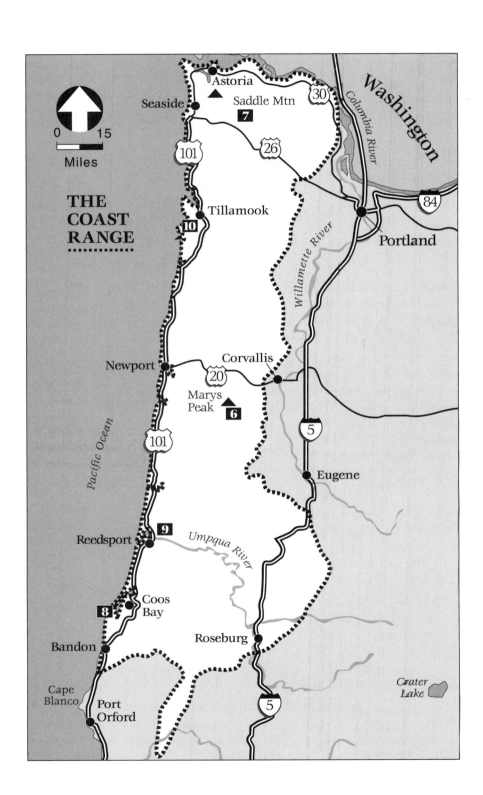

Hike 6

MARYS PEAK

PILLOW LAVAS AND SEAMOUNTS

An unususal intrusive formation caps Marys Peak and provides a grand view of the Coast Range and the Cascades.

DISTANCE ■ **9.6 miles**

ELEVATION ■ **2,500 to 4,097 feet**

DIFFICULTY ■ **Strenuous**

TOPOGRAPHIC MAPS ■ **Marys Peak, Alsea**

GEOLOGIC MAP ■ **9**

PRECAUTIONS ■ **Poison oak is present in some places. Carry water.**

FOR INFORMATION ■ **Alsea Ranger District**

About the Landscape: For a quick trip to the seafloor, nothing beats the Siletz River volcanics on Marys Peak. These are perhaps the best example of *pillow lavas* that can be found anywhere. Their globby forms and glassy exterior indicate that the molten lava chilled and solidified very quickly. Although they are invisible along the uphill-bound trail, these rocks are beautifully exposed in a quarry near Marys Peak Road (USFS 30).

A resistant, 700-foot-thick gabbro *sill* (a flat-topped and flat-bottomed intrusion) caps Marys Peak. The rock is dark gray-green and has the same overall composition as basalt. It intruded into the sedimentary rocks (Flournoy Formation) that overlie the 56-million-year-old pillow lavas, forcing its way as a molten mass in between sedimentary layers. The Marys Peak sill is about 30 million years in age. It has many relatives scattered through the Coast Range, including rocks at the summits of Roman Nose, Fanno Peak, and Elk Mountain.

Trail Guide: This loop hike rises 1,000 feet in 3 miles, passing through an area of huge noble fir before reaching the summit of Marys Peak at 4,097 feet. The downward route reveals the Marys Peak sill and the sandstones of the Flournoy Formation. Pillow lavas are well exposed in a quarry off Marys Peak Road (USFS 30).

To reach the trailhead, from Corvallis take Highway 20 west for about 5 miles and turn south on Oregon Highway 34 (Alsea Highway). Drive 9 miles west on Highway 34 to USFS 30 (Marys Peak Road) and turn right. Follow the winding road upward for 3.5 miles until you reach a turnout on the left which provides an overview to the west. A gated gravel road here leads 0.25 mile west to an exquisite exposure of pillow lava in an abandoned quarry.

From this stop, continue on Marys Peak Road another 2 miles to milepost 5.5. Turn right into the parking area for the East Ridge trailhead (trail

Oligocene pillow basalts and lava tubes in a roadcut near Marys Peak

1324). The trail leads straight up a gentle grade through mixed fir and then noble fir forest. About 1 mile along the walk, the East Ridge trail meets trail 1313. Turn left, upslope, and continue 1 mile on trail 1324. After another switchbacking hike through forest, the trail meets the Summit Loop Trail (trail 1350). Take trail 1350 upward to cross Marys Peak Road in 0.5 mile, reaching the summit in about another 0.5 mile. From the summit, you have an excellent view of the Coast Range.

Several paths lead downward through Marys Peak meadow, which receives about 100 inches of rainfall annually and supports an ecological collage of plants adapted to extreme climates. The best route is Meadow Edge Trail (trail 1325), which can be found by retracing the Summit Loop Trail (1350) back to just before its junction with Marys Peak Road.

Follow the Meadow Edge Trail 1.6 miles downhill to Marys Peak campground. Then follow Marys Peak Road 3 miles back to the East Ridge trailhead (be wary of traffic). Along the way (1.5 miles from the campground), you will find an excellent exposure of the Marys Peak gabbro sill at Parker Falls. The fine-grained texture of this rock indicates that it was fairly near the surface (perhaps less than 1,000 feet beneath the seafloor) when it intruded the seafloor sediments and cooled. Its composition is similar to the pillow lavas exposed in the quarry, but it is a much younger formation (about 30 million years old as opposed to 56 million years). At 2.5 miles beyond the campground, roadcuts reveal the alternating sandstones and shales of the Flournoy Formation. These Eocene rocks, which lie just above the pillow lavas, are *turbidites*. Such alternating sandstone and shale sequences are created when a storm or earthquake stirs up nearshore sands into a dense cloud of sediment. That cloud of sediment moves rapidly downslope, spreading coarse sands into deeper water, where the sand is deposited in a layer. The finer-grained sediment transported with it settles to the seafloor more gradually and becomes the shale atop the sandstone layers. Close scrutiny of these beds reveals sedimentary structures such as cross-bedding and the tracks of pebbles or sticks dragged along by the fast-moving sand. The remaining half-mile hike back to the trailhead follows an easy, curving downhill stretch of road.

Hike 7

SADDLE MOUNTAIN

THE 300-MILE-LONG BASALT FLOW

This hike tours basalt that flowed more than 250 miles from eastern Washington to the Oregon coast.

DISTANCE ■ 4.6 miles

ELEVATION ■ 1,600 to 3,280 feet

DIFFICULTY ■ Strenuous

TOPOGRAPHIC MAP ■ Saddle Mountain

GEOLOGIC MAP ■ 1

PRECAUTIONS ■ Carry water. Upper portions of the trail are slick paths on narrow ledges. Avoid the summits in wet conditions.

FOR INFORMATION ■ Saddle Mountain State Park

About the Landscape: Saddle Mountain's dark peaks are composed of a single thick flow of Columbia River basalt. It is mind-boggling that the source of this lava flow is a basalt dike in eastern Washington, about 250 miles away. The flow at the top of Saddle Mountain is part of the Frenchman Springs flows in the Wanapum group of Columbia River basalts. These erupted about 14.5 million years ago, as the major Columbia River basalt eruptions began to dwindle.

GEOLOGIC TIMETABLE 2: THE COAST RANGE		
Five significant events that shaped the landscape		
Millions of years ago	**Geologic era**	**Geologic event**
0.0003 (300 years)	Holocene	Most recent great subduction zone earthquake; quakes of magnitude 8 or 9 occur an average of every 600 years
14	Miocene	Columbia River basalt flows reach the coast
20–25	Oligocene	Seamounts accreted to Oregon create the Coast Range
36	Oligocene	Sills intruded off the coast; these rocks will eventually form summits of Marys Peak and other mountains
40–50	Eocene	Pillow lavas erupt under the ocean to form seamounts that today form much of Coast Range; seafloor sediment, including the Tyee Formation, deposited

The peaks of Saddle Mountain are corrugated. The basalt breaks away from the cliffs in little, irregular chunks. Instead of columns, the cliffs bear a lattice-work of cracks and thin bands, occasionally punctuated by a thick, solid dike shooting its way to the top. The type of cracks, or joints, that developed in many of the later Columbia River basalt flows—like the Frenchman Springs flow here or the Pomona flow that forms Crown Point in the Columbia River Gorge—is decidedly different from the stately columns of the Columbia River Gorge.

The Frenchman Springs flow, nearing the Miocene coast as it ran through a river valley, cooled rapidly and explosively as it encountered the sea. The result was *breccia*—broken, fragmented basalt. The vertical dikes that cut through Saddle Mountain's basalt cliffs are not standard intrusive dikes that carried lava from a deep magma chamber to the surface. Instead, they were generated by still-fluid portions of the same basalt flow forcing its way *down* through the broken, brecciated basalt. The process was rather like squeezing caulking into cracks or pressure-sealing concrete. Other Columbia River basalt flows that reached the coast also produced such *invasive* dikes. They include the semicircular basalt dikes exposed at low tide north of Otter Rocks, and the basalts near Depoe Bay.

Trail Guide: The steadily rising trail to the summit of Saddle Mountain remains in second-growth forest for most of its length. Riotous vegetation covers the sedimentary rocks—primarily marine sandstones and siltstones, about 15 to 20 million years old—at the base of Saddle Mountain.

The trail begins at Saddle Mountain State Park. From Portland, take US 26 west toward Astoria. About 4.8 miles west of the David Douglas Wayside, turn north onto Saddle Mountain Road. A sign to Saddle Mountain

State Park marks this road. The park is 7 miles north at the road's end.

The trail begins at the east side of the parking area. About 1 mile along the steadily climbing trail, trees thin and the bare double peaks of Saddle Mountain loom ahead. The remaining 1.3 miles is a winding climb to the north and highest summit. A 0.25 mile portion of the trail threads a narrow ridge with only a cable as a handhold.

At the summit, the broken nature of Saddle Mountain's venturesome Columbia River basalt is evident. Fresh black basalt is rare; most rock is a glued-together basaltic rubble. The view of the sea and the Coast Range is a great reward for the climb. Return as you came.

COAST TRAIL

Hike 8

SUNSET BAY TO SOUTH COVE

At low tide, rhythmically bedded sandstones and shales are exposed along the beach at Cape Arago.

DISTANCE ■ **4 miles one way**

ELEVATION ■ **0 to 120 feet**

DIFFICULTY ■ **Easy**

TOPOGRAPHIC MAPS ■ **Cape Arago, Charleston**

GEOLOGIC MAP ■ **10**

PRECAUTIONS ■ **Be watchful for sneaker waves—high waves that appear without warning. This hike should be done at low tide. It can be done year-round. Provide a shuttle vehicle at Cape Arago State Park unless you wish to double the length of the hike by retracing your route.**

FOR INFORMATION ■ **Sunset Bay State Park, Shore Acres State Park, Cape Arago State Park**

About the Landscape: Sedimentary rocks and wave-cut terraces decorate the coastline at Shore Acres State Park, just south of Sunset Bay State Park. The yellow sandstones of Cape Arago and Sunset Bay are part of the Coaledo Formation. These rocks are Eocene in age, about 45 million years old. They were deposited in relatively shallow water as tidal or lagoonal sands. The name "Coaledo Formation" stems from the presence of coal in some layers of the formation.

Trail Guide: The Coast Trail weaves from cliff to beach to outcrop to road, providing a 4-mile walk between Sunset Bay and Cape Arago State Parks, with occasional descents to the beach. The layered sedimentary rocks of Sunset Bay Beach and Cape Arago beautifully display the patterns of

Sandstones and clay and calcite concretions at Shore Acres State Park
(Photo courtesy Oregon Dept. of Transportation)

Eocene ocean currents in swirling sand. Low tide permits close-up examination of the rocks and is the best time to explore here. Sea lions at Simpson Reef provide noisy accompaniment to the waves' roar.

Reach Sunset Bay State Park in about 12 miles from Coos Bay by driving west on the Empire–Coos Bay Highway to Empire, then south through Charleston on the Cape Arago Highway. Or, from Highway 101 5 miles north of Bandon, bear west on Seven Devils Road—a shortcut to Charleston—and turn south to Sunset Bay State Park.

The best views of the patterned sedimentary structures are found in the rocks around Sunset Bay. Well-exposed sandstone layers emerge from the sand south of the bay and also on its north side. A walk at low tide reveals world-class cross-bedding patterns in the stone.

After exploring the area around Sunset Bay, take the Coast Trail south from the south end of Sunset Bay Beach. South of Sunset Bay, rounded forms known as *concretions* appear in the rocks. These concretions are concentrations of clay and calcite cement that collect around a fossil or some other impurity in the rock. This process occurs after the sediment is deposited, and usually before it becomes solid stone. Several small faults cut through the rocks here, and are easy to spot in the barren outcrops.

In 1 mile, the trail splits; take the Coast Trail to the right, though both trails lead to Shore Acres State Park in another 1 mile. From Shore Acres continue on the Coast Trail to Simpson Beach and on to Simpson Reef Viewpoint in another 1.25 miles. This is the end of the Coast Trail. From here walk about 0.5 mile south along the Cape Arago Highway to Cape Arago State Park.

An approach to the beach at Cape Arago State Park provides excellent close-up views of patterned sandstones. The Cape Arago South Cove Trail begins at the picnic area just past the south end of the Cape Arago parking lot, dropping over the edge of the cliff and winding abruptly downslope to the beach below in 0.25 mile. The outcrops and tide pools are north and west of the beach. When you are finished exploring, walk back up the 0.25-mile South Cove trail to the trailhead and your shuttle vehicle.

TAHKENITCH DUNES TRAIL

Hike

9

OREGON DUNES LOOP

This short walk through a dune field to the ocean showcases dune forms, a lake, and, usually, plenty of solitude.

DISTANCE ■ 4-mile loop

ELEVATION ■ 0 to 100 feet

DIFFICULTY ■ Easy

TOPOGRAPHIC MAP ■ Tahkenitch Creek

GEOLOGIC MAP ■ 1

PRECAUTIONS ■ Protect against wind-blown sand. Avoid disturbing snowy plover habitat; keep dogs on leash.

FOR INFORMATION ■ Oregon Dunes National Recreation Area, Tahkenitch Lake State Park

About the Landscape: Most dunal forms at Oregon Dunes National Recreation Area are *longitudinal dunes*. These long, narrow dunes form in areas where the wind blows from different directions seasonally. Here, wind blows generally from south to north in the winter, and from north to south in the summer. The classic, crescent-shaped *barchan dunes* that we find in many deserts are formed by wind from a steady or constant direction, and are absent from this part of Oregon Dunes.

Trail Guide: From Reedsport, drive 5 miles north on Highway 101 to the Tahkenitch Lake State Park campground and picnic area. The trailhead is at the south end of this area.

From the trailhead, walk about 0.25 mile south on a short access trail, then turn right onto Tahkenitch Dune Trail. A 0.5-mile walk through a forest built on sand dunes brings you to the brink of dunes. This is a *deflation basin*, where sand is temporarily dropped, only to be picked up by the wind and moved on. Higher dunes border the area to the south and north. It is a great place to observe dune forms and the process of dune construction—and destruction.

A brisk 1-mile walk across the dunes brings you to a line of pine trees and a narrow pine forest. Large wooden posts mark the trail across these dunes. At the west edge of the trees, turn south and hike about 1.5 miles

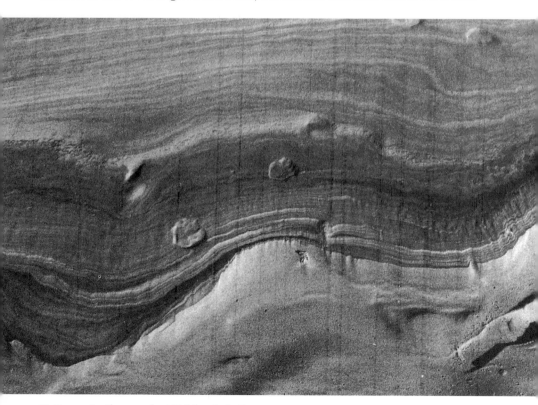

Patterns in the sand at Tahkenitch Dunes

to Threemile Lake, a freshwater lake perched precariously on the sand dunes. The lake's fresh water is protected from invasion of salt water by an apron of several small fresh-water creeks.

The trail loops around the lake, crossing through snowy plover habitat and returning to the junction with the 0.25-mile access trail back to the trailhead.

NETARTS BAY

EVIDENCE FOR EARTHQUAKES

Marshes and terraces around Netarts Bay provide evidence for periodic great earthquakes and tidal waves.

DISTANCE ■ **2 miles; 10 miles to end of Netarts spit**
ELEVATION ■ **0 feet**
DIFFICULTY ■ **Easy**
TOPOGRAPHIC MAPS ■ **Netarts, Sand Lake**
GEOLOGIC MAP ■ **1**
PRECAUTIONS ■ **Beware of sneaker waves on beach hikes.**
FOR INFORMATION ■ **Cape Lookout State Park**

About the Landscape: The flat, unobtrusive marshes at the south end of the Netarts spit and Netarts Bay are among the most significant geologic localities in Oregon and are classic examples of a salt marsh ecosystem. Plant cover includes tufted hairgrass and several reeds. In the soils below these plants, dark layers of peat represent down-dropped and drowned salt-marsh vegetation. Above the dark peat, you can often find a thin deposit of coarse sand. What happened in these salt marshes to produce such a deposit?

This is the footprint of a *tsunami,* or tidal wave. Each peat layer and the associated sandy cap represents a great earthquake. The tidal marsh at Netarts Bay, as well as other tidal marshes up and down the Washington and Oregon coastlines, provides a record of synchronous, sudden, and periodic *subsidence,* or sinking—a drowned salt marsh covered and sealed immediately by the sandy deposit of a huge, incoming wave.

Netarts Bay is a perfect location to discover the relationship between salt marsh subsidence and earthquakes because it is protected from storm-related sand deposits by the elegant spit. The small stream that feeds the bay is extremely unlikely to transport coarse sands into the salt marsh. The underlying and surrounding basalt headlands on Cape Lookout

Thin layers of peat and sand in the marsh at Netarts Bay provide evidence of earthquakes.

and Cape Meares provide a protected and otherwise stable platform for the marsh.

This record of salt marsh subsidence and earthquakes was first explored by Curt Peterson in the early 1980s here in Netarts Bay. By carbon-dating the drowned peat layers, Peterson produced a timetable of great earthquakes—magnitude 8 or 9 (similar to the 1964 Alaska earthquake)—on the Oregon coast at Netarts Bay. The record was strikingly synchronous with the records of earthquakes based on other criteria. Overall, the record at Netarts indicates major, magnitude 8 or 9 earthquakes occurred at an average of every 600 years: 440, 700, 1,450, 2,040, 2,820, and 3,300 years ago.

Trail Guide: Low tide is the best time to undertake this adventure along Netarts spit. Dunes, ripplemarks, and wildlife provide entertainment and diversion. Expect wet feet in this marshland.

The hike begins at Cape Lookout State Park, on the Three Capes Scenic Loop road west of Highway 101 south of the town of Netarts. At the day-use parking lot, find beach access and walk north along the Netarts Spit beach. Detour around the campground to the marsh (behind camp-site B-44). This area is wet. At low tide, you can see dark layers of peat exposed in the sides of channels.

Proceed along the trail about 0.25 mile and go through a gate, then follow a gravel road north along the spit. About 0.75 mile along this road, walk approximately 100 feet eastward through the marsh grasses to the sharp, 3-foot-high bank above the marsh waterway that appears directly ahead. Although this looks suspiciously like a fault scarp, it is not. Waves and currents carved this bank.

Scrutiny of this bank reveals two thin, dark, organic-rich layers. The up-permost is capped by a thin layer of fine sand. The dark peat-rich layers are the remnant of drowned salt-marsh vegetation. The sand is a tsunami deposit—the relatively coarse sediment deposited by a tidal wave that swept over the marsh immediately following the earthquake. The peat layers have been radio-carbon dated. The lower layer is about 700 years old; the upper layer is about 440 years old.

From this bank, turn around and retrace your path back to the trailhead for a round trip of 2 miles. For a longer hike, Netarts spit invites another 4 miles of hiking to the end.

Chapter 3.
THE WILLAMETTE VALLEY

Trail on Spencers Butte

The Willamette Valley began its life 40 million years ago as seafloor off the early Cascades. Scotts Mills, Silver Falls, and Sweet Home would have been seaports. Today, the rocks associated with the old seafloor and coastline are deeply buried beneath Ice Age and younger sediments in the valley bottom. Faults and earthquakes are sculpting the valley's modern topography.

The oldest rocks exposed in the Willamette Valley are the isolated buttes—Skinner Butte, Spencers Butte, the Coburg Hills, and Knox Butte—found in its southern half. Most geologists believe that these intrusions, lava flows, and small volcanos, which average 30 million years in age, originated in the Western Cascades. In the late Oligocene the Willamette Valley was covered by the sea, but by the early Miocene, about 20 million years ago, the rocks of the Coast Range "docked" with the continent and were uplifted, creating the mountains and elevating the valley above the waves. Lavas from the nearby Western Cascades flowed over the new land, which was punctuated by a few small volcanos. By 15 million years ago, the valley floor was dry ground.

Columbia River basalt flows followed the river's ancestral channel into the Willamette Valley and west to the coast, reaching the sea at what is now Newport. Some spread out in the Willamette lowland. Today, Columbia River basalts form the cliffs at Oregon City, Portland's Forest Park and West Hills, as well as the South Salem Hills, Amity Hills, and Eola Hills, and elsewhere in the northern Willamette Valley.

The Portland area has its share of volcanic buttes, including Mount Tabor, Rocky Butte, and Mount Sylvan. These and dozens more local buttes are part of the Boring Lavas, named for the town of Boring. They developed 1.5 to 2.5 million years ago as faulting pulled the Portland basin apart, and may have opened the Willamette Valley to the south as well.

In the Pleistocene, the Willamette Valley periodically became a huge lake. Water from an ice-dammed lake in Montana was unleashed repeatedly and swept down the ancient Columbia River channel. These so-called Missoula floods carried glacial ice and created a dam across the Columbia near what is now the town of St. Helens. Silt-laden water flooded the Willamette Valley to depths of 200 feet (at an elevation of 310 feet above sea level). Even today, small clusters of ice-rafted granite boulders appear in fields and backyards throughout the valley. An Oregon state park—Erratic Wayside—is dedicated to a huge boulder transported from Montana on such a raft of ice.

Two major fault zones are pulling the Portland Basin apart: the Portland Hills fault on the west defines Portland's West Hills, while multiple faults cut through the Gresham area. Earthquakes along these faults, and from

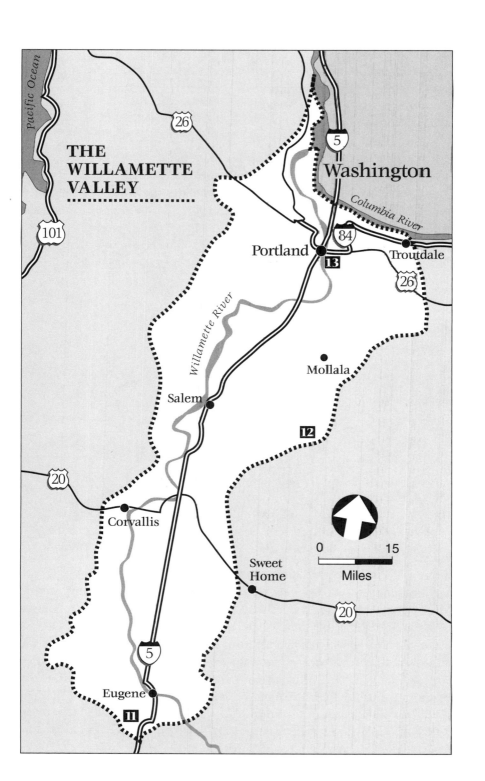

THE WILLAMETTE VALLEY

Pacific Ocean

101

US 26

Washington

Columbia River

84

Portland **13**

Troutdale

US 26

Willamette River

Mollala

Salem

12

US 20

Corvallis

Sweet Home

0   15
Miles

US 20

I-5

Eugene

11

the subduction zone beneath, have rattled Portland frequently. These quakes include magnitude 4.5 in 1953, 4.5 in 1961, and 5.6 in 1963. Geologists estimate that a magnitude 6 quake strikes the Portland area about once every 100 to 150 years, and a quake greater than 6.5 strikes every 800 to 900 years.

Another fault system, the Mount Angel fault, runs across the Willamette Valley south of Salem. In 1990 a cluster of barely noticed earthquakes (magnitude 1 and 2) tickled Woodburn. In 1992 the Scotts Mills earthquake, magnitude 5.6, on these faults cracked the state capitol dome, damaged 90 buildings and a major bridge, and caused more than $28 million in property damage. This Mount Angel fault system is part of a series of faults that are opening, extending, and rotating the Willamette Valley. Similar fault systems may await detection south of Salem.

Hike

11

SPENCERS BUTTE

The Willamette Valley's Orphan

Hike to the top of a large basaltic butte in the southern Willamette Valley.

DISTANCE ■ **1.5 miles**

ELEVATION ■ **1,250 to 2,054 feet**

DIFFICULTY ■ **Moderate**

TOPOGRAPHIC MAPS ■ Creswell, Fox Hollow

GEOLOGIC MAP ■ 1

PRECAUTIONS ■ Keep dogs on leash. Carry water. Poison oak is prolific in open areas. The trail is eroded and steep in many places.

FOR INFORMATION ■ Spencers Butte Park (Lane County Parks Division)

About the Landscape: The dark, pointed buttes in the Willamette Valley, including the Coburg Hills northeast of Eugene, are composed of basalt. These rocks are 24 to 32 million years old. Most are shallow intrusions or possibly the eroded remnants of lava flows. Only one, Peterson Butte, 4 miles southwest of Lebanon, seems to have erupted. Peterson Butte has a central volcanic vent with twelve radiating dikes extending outwards in all directions from the center of the butte into the sediments. Skinner Butte and Spencers Butte both seem to be remnant lava flows or shallow intrusions.

Trail Guide: This short hike takes you to the top of Spencers Butte, at 2,054 feet the highest isolated basaltic butte in the Willamette Valley.

To reach Spencers Butte Park, from 6th Street in downtown Eugene drive south on Willamette Street. The park and parking lot are on the left in 5 miles.

The trail begins with concrete steps and immediately bears left uphill. For most of its 0.75-mile upward-bound grade, this trail traverses a forest. The open summit, however, reveals the basalts that support Spencers Butte. These solid, dark rocks are coarse-grained and display only coarse

Basaltic outcrops mark the summit of Spencers Butte.

columnar jointing, suggesting that Spencers Butte represents a shallow intrusion rather than a lava flow. The landscape to the north is pimpled with other basaltic buttes, including the Coburg Hills to the northeast. Retrace your path down the butte to the trailhead.

SILVER CREEK CANYON TRAIL

The Ancient Cascade Shoreline

The scenery and multitude of waterfalls and basaltic outcrops beckon and creeks follow some very active earthquake faults.

DISTANCE ■ 9-mile loop

ELEVATION ■ 1,100 to 1,500 feet

DIFFICULTY ■ Moderate

TOPOGRAPHIC MAPS ■ Drake Crossing, Stout Mtn., Lyons

GEOLOGIC MAPS ■ 11, 12

PRECAUTIONS ■ This is a day-use fee area.

FOR INFORMATION ■ Silver Falls State Park

About the Landscape: On a warm summer day when you are torn between going to the mountains or heading for the beach, do both. Go to Silver Falls State Park and pitch your beach umbrella on a 25-million-year-old shoreline where waterfalls echo long-vanished waves from an ancient ocean beach.

Long ago, Oregon's shore ran along the western base of the Cascade Mountains. The Coast Range was not far offshore. The coastline here was rocky, probably a warmer version of the modern Oregon coast north of Newport. Headlands and seastacks composed of basalts from the Cascades jutted into the ocean.

The sedimentary rocks deposited on that long-ago beach are known as the Scotts Mills Formation. They extend along the west side of the Willamette Valley from Silverton north to Mollala. They make fleeting guest appearances beneath the waterfalls at Silver Falls State Park.

The rocks that support the waterfalls are Columbia River basalt. These basalt flows and the gravels of their contemporary streams buried and preserved the forest that originally grew here. Today, the waterfalls that proliferate at Silver Falls are a reminder that the Columbia River basalt is resistant to erosion.

Trail Guide: For all its seeming isolation, popular Silver Falls State Park sports a lodge, a restaurant, and a long history of development.

From Salem, drive east on Highway 22 about 6 miles, turn north on Highway 214, and follow it about 16 miles to Silver Falls State Park.

The best place to begin this loop hike is from South Falls Day-use Area A; a path descends to South Falls, the most popular falls at the park. A sloping trail and stairway lets you explore all around this falls, including walking behind the cascading water. Behind the falls and beneath the basalts you will find the shy exposures of the 25-million-year-old beach sands.

From South Falls, the main loop trail continues counterclockwise on the canyon rim to Winter Falls, Twin Falls, and North Falls. North Falls, 3 miles from South Falls, provides the best view of the Scotts Mills Formation sandstones below the Columbia River basalts.

Other falls offer views of basalt columns and basalt breccia up close and personal. From North Falls, the loop continues to Middle North Falls, Drake Falls, and Lower South Falls, at 9 miles from the starting point. Completion of the loop hike is an all-day project.

The Upper North Falls at Silver Falls State Park plummets over two thin basalt flows.

ICE AGE FLOODS ON THE COLUMBIA

During the last part of the Ice Age, 12,000 years ago, the most catastrophic floods ever documented on earth swept repeatedly from Montana across central and eastern Oregon and down the Columbia River, scouring bedrock and depositing glacial erratics and deep mud. These floods are known as the Missoula floods. There were at least 120 separate flood events of differing duration and magnitude.

In the waning Pleistocene, a lobe of the continental ice sheet in northern Idaho periodically formed an ice dam across Montana's Clark Fork River. The resulting lake in the Missoula River valley was 950 feet deep. Wave-cut benches still form parallel lines on the hill around Missoula. Periodically, the pressure of water lifted or broke this ice dam, sending billions of gallons of glacial meltwater surging westward. These floods stripped the landscape of eastern Washington (the channeled scablands) down to the bedrock, and polished and widened the Columbia River Gorge. The water flowed even with the top of Wallula Gap and Crown Point, and flooded the Willamette Valley to a depth of about 300 feet. Huge icebergs more than 100 feet long rafted granite boulders from Anaconda, Montana, to the Willamette Valley. Much of the Willamette Valley's fertile soil is a gift of these floods.

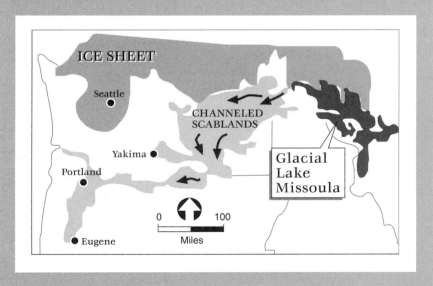

GEOLOGIC TIMETABLE 3: THE WILLAMETTE VALLEY

Five significant events that shaped the landscape

Millions of years ago	Geologic era	Geologic event
0.00001 (1994–96)	Holocene	Scotts Mills earthquake continues the faulting that is presently sculpting the landscape; floods of 1995–96 also modify landscape
0.012–0.015	Pleistocene	Missoula (Bretz) floods flood valley and deposit sediment
1–3	Pleistocene and Pliocene	Boring Lavas erupt in Portland basin
14–15	Miocene	Columbia River basalts cover central parts of valley
24–32	Oligocene	Basalt flows and sills of Willamette Valley buttes erupt

Hike 13

MOUNT TABOR

THE NOT SO BORING LAVAS

A walk up a small, urban volcano provides a glimpse into its past and a view of the Portland Basin and its fault zones.

DISTANCE ■ 1 mile

ELEVATION ■ 150 to 600 feet

DIFFICULTY ■ Easy

TOPOGRAPHIC MAP ■ Mount Tabor

GEOLOGIC MAPS ■ 13–20

PRECAUTIONS ■ None

FOR INFORMATION ■ Portland Parks and Recreation Department

About the Landscape: Most small buttes that pimple Portland's landscape are bantam-weight volcanos that erupted basalt between 2.5 and 1.5 million years ago. They are known as Boring Lavas, named for the small town of Boring 20 miles southeast of Portland, where the vents are abundant and the basalts are thick. The Boring Lavas include at least thirty-two eruptive vents, including Portland landmarks like Mount Tabor and Rocky Butte, as well as flows atop the Portland Hills and exposed along Interstate 205 near Oregon City.

Despite their youth, much of the Boring Lavas has been erased by time and floods. Although many volcanos still have a low cone shape, they were scoured by the Missoula floods about 15,000 to 12,000 years ago. The Boring Lavas seem related to the pull-apart, extensional nature of the Portland Basin. In this thin, faulted crust, basalts like the Boring Lavas rise rapidly to the surface and erupt easily.

Layers of pumice and ash mark the eruptive vent that created Mount Tabor

Trail Guide: The excursion up Mount Tabor is a popular summer evening activity in southeast Portland. Walkers, joggers, cyclers, skateboarders, rollerbladers, dogs, and even cats on leashes make the pilgrimage to the top and back.

The walk to the summit begins in Portland's east side on NE 64th Avenue (other routes are available as well). The two important stops on the short walk are the basketball court-amphitheater and the tree-shrouded summit.

The amphitheater at about 0.25 mile from the NE 64th Avenue park entry provides a revealing cross section of a Boring Lavas vent. The upper portion is *scoria*, lava and *lava bombs* in volcanic cinders. Below this, a light-colored, layered rock is made up of ash and pebbles from the underlying Troutdale gravels, now buried several hundred feet below the volcano. Boring Lavas are about 200 feet thick around the Mount Tabor cone.

The summit of Mount Tabor provides leaf-fringed glimpses to the north, south, and west. To the north, Rocky Butte is visible. To the south, more small volcanos, including Mount Scott and Powell Butte, appear. Boring Lavas that erupted atop Sylvan Heights are visible to the west. On the west side of Portland, the Portland Hills escarpment frames the Portland Hills fault.

Chapter 4.

THE COLUMBIA RIVER GORGE

Falls at Warren Creek, Columbia River Gorge

The Columbia River Gorge was forged by a 30-million-year feud between fire and water. From the Miocene to the present, the rivalry between a powerful river and persistent volcanos built landscapes and wore them away, carved canyons and filled them. The landscape you see from Crown Point or Larch Mountain strikes a delicate balance between the earth's motile surface and its churning interior.

The Columbia River has shepherded water across Oregon for at least the last 20 million years. During that time, its channel has migrated fitfully northward. Some 25 million years ago, the Columbia ran just north of where Mount Jefferson stands and reached the sea at Stayton. When the Coast Range finally reared its head above the waves about 18 million years ago, the Columbia extended its channel west, embracing the sea again near Newport.

The Columbia River provided an easy path westward for Columbia River basalt lavas: they followed the river. And they also filled the canyon, forcing the stream farther and farther north. By 14 million years ago, the Columbia River had been edged almost to its present channel by lavas and the rising Coast Range and Cascades. Its course, known as the Bridal Veil channel, lay just south of the present canyon.

But 4 million years ago lavas and mudflows from the High Cascades and the Boring Lavas (see chapter 3, The Willamette Valley, hike 13, Mount Tabor) began to fill the Bridal Veil channel. By 2 million years ago, the Columbia had doggedly cut yet another channel through the rising Cascades, creating the deep canyon that we see today. The remnants of older channels are exposed in the sidewalls of the gorge.

Gravels transported by the Columbia River during the last 10 million years are called the Troutdale Formation. They are found throughout the Gorge and the Portland Basin.

As the Ice Age waned 15,000 years ago, volcanos quieted. The Columbia flexed its fluid muscles again. As a result of 120 huge floods of ice-dammed lake water from Montana, the river widened its gorge, polished and steepened its sides, and spread sediment across the Willamette Valley.

Near Bonneville, humans have built a great dam 80 feet high across the Columbia. But seven centuries before the Army Corps of Engineers and bulldozers were around, a landslide from the north side of the river cleaved the raw face of Table Mountain and built a dam 270 feet high across this river. Forests as far east as The Dalles were drowned as the lake filled behind the dam. For months before the river topped the dam, Indian tribes were able to cross the river dryshod; once the river topped the dam it resulted in the Cascades of the Columbia. The Salish and Chinook peoples

COLUMBIA RIVER BASALT

The Pacific Northwest is the home of a world-class *flood basalt*. From 17.5 to less than 12 million years ago, the Columbia River basalts poured across Oregon and Washington. These lavas, erupted from long cracks or fissures in eastern Oregon, eastern Washington, and western Idaho, were so fluid that they did not form volcanos. Instead, they spread across the landscape like syrup on pancakes, filling depressions and river valleys and covering more than 63,000 square miles. Some of the later flows followed the course of the Columbia River to the sea. Today they are about 15,000 feet thick beneath Richland and Pasco, Washington.

The Columbia River basalts erupted in four discrete pulses. The first basalts, called *Imnaha basalts,* 17 million years ago flowed from fissures now found in the Wallowa Mountains. Most of the Columbia River basalts (85 percent by volume) erupted between 16.5 and 15.5 million years ago and are named the *Grande Ronde basalts.* The last two eruptive episodes were the *Wanapum basalts* from 15.5 to 14.5 million years ago, and the *Saddle Mountain basalts* from 14.5 to as recently as 6 million years ago.

Extensive flood basalts related to the Columbia River basalts erupted in central Oregon as well. The oldest, known as the *Picture Gorge basalts,* erupted 16 million years ago from fissures near what is today downtown Monument, and are elegantly displayed in Picture Gorge. The other group, known as the *Prineville basalts,* are found between Prineville and Brothers, and are well exposed at Prineville Reservoir.

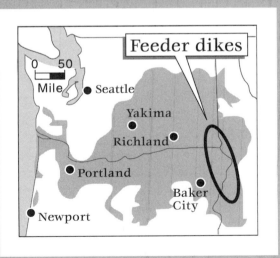

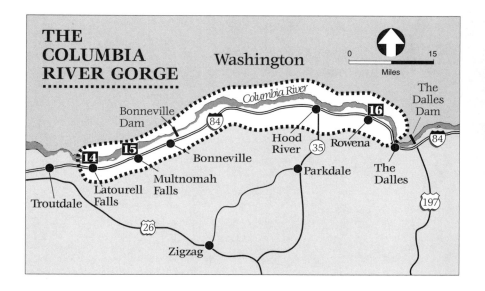

THE COLUMBIA RIVER GORGE

Washington

Columbia River

Bonneville Dam

The Dalles Dam

16

Hood River

Rowena

The Dalles

Bonneville

Parkdale

Multnomah Falls

14 **15**

Latourell Falls

Troutdale

Zigzag

0   15
Miles

remember this natural dam and the dry-footed crossing in their stories of the Bridge of the Gods. Today, landslides and the Columbia River remain active forces in the Gorge.

LATOURELL FALLS

Hike 14

A Tale of Three Basalts

Explore three different types of Columbia River basalts as well as the sedimentary rocks beneath these oldest basalts.

DISTANCE ■ 1 mile

ELEVATION ■ 250 to 650 feet

DIFFICULTY ■ Moderate

TOPOGRAPHIC MAP ■ Bridal Veil

GEOLOGIC MAP ■ 1

PRECAUTIONS ■ Major flooding in the winters of 1995–97 severely damaged the trail, and limited access along the Columbia Gorge Scenic Highway (Crown Point); check locally before planning this hike.

FOR INFORMATION ■ Guy W. Talbot State Park

About the Landscape: Three different kinds of Columbia River basalts are exposed at Latourell Falls: the Grande Ronde basalts, the Frenchman Springs flow, and the Priest Rapids flow. The Grande Ronde flow at the base

Opposite: *Upper Latourell Falls*

GEOLOGIC TIMETABLE 4: THE COLUMBIA RIVER GORGE

Five significant events that shaped the landscape

Millions of years ago	Geologic era	Geologic event
0.0006	Holocene	Bridge of the Gods landslide dams the Columbia
0.012–0.015	Pleistocene	Missoula (Bretz) floods scour the Columbia River Gorge
0.730–present	Pleistocene and Recent	High Cascade eruptions modify river course and sediments
2–5	Pliocene	Columbia River flows in the Bridal Veil channel south of its present course; Troutdale Formation deposited
6–15	Miocene	Columbia River basalt flows follow river's course and also build landscape and shift river's position

of the falls is the oldest, about 15.5 million years in age. The Frenchman Springs flow above the falls originated northwest of Pendleton. These basalts were so voluminous that they clogged the Columbia's southern channel, forcing the river to move north almost to its present position about 14 million years ago. Frenchman Springs basalts are fine-grained rocks and usually display blocky or poorly developed joints.

The uppermost basalt at Latourell Falls is a Priest Rapids flow. This basalt flow erupted in west-central Idaho, flowing more than 300 miles to this location about 14 million years ago. These rocks are extremely fine grained. Like the Frenchman Springs flow before it, the Priest Rapids flow filled the Columbia's canyon, forcing the river north again.

Trail Guide: This relatively easy short loop hike leads through the lush forest of the Columbia Gorge to two major waterfalls, providing intimate views of three major types of Columbia River basalt and an example of the oldest rock in the Columbia River Gorge.

From Multnomah Falls, follow the old Columbia River Scenic Highway 6 miles west to the turnout for Latourell Falls. At the southwest end of the parking lot, a paved trail leads past a gray outcrop. Part of the Oligocene Skamania volcanics, this outcrop represents some of the oldest rocks (25-30 million years) in the Columbia River Gorge. This short, 0.25 mile, path provides a closeup view of Latourell Creek's plunge over several flows of elegantly columned Grande Ronde Columbia River basalt, which is 16 million-years old.

Return to the parking lot and take the main trail that leads upslope to an overview of Latourell Falls. Continue past the overview about 200 yards to the top of the lower falls, where the trail splits. One path leads along the east side of the creek, the other takes the west bank. Both lead to upper Latourell Falls in a level 0.5-mile walk. Visible along the way are outcrops of Frenchman Springs Columbia River basalt (about 15 million years old). At the upper falls, the creek pours over the Priest Rapids basalt, which, at about 14 million years, is the second youngest Columbia River basalt flow exposed in the Gorge. This basalt displays well developed columnar joints. Return along the opposite side of the creek if you wish to see slightly different scenery.

Hike 15

MULTNOMAH FALLS TO LARCH MOUNTAIN

Two Basalts and a Mountain

This long climb crosses eleven Columbia River basalt flows and leads to a small basalt shield volcano.

DISTANCE ■ **14 miles**

ELEVATION ■ **150 to 4,056 feet**

DIFFICULTY ■ **Strenuous**

TOPOGRAPHIC MAPS ■ **Bridal Veil, Multnomah Falls**

GEOLOGIC MAP ■ **21**

PRECAUTIONS ■ **Flooding and debris slides during the winters of 1995–97 damaged this trail; check at Multnomah Lodge before proceeding.**

FOR INFORMATION ■ **Multnomah Lodge, USFS**

About the Landscape: Eleven flows of Columbia River basalt are exposed at Multnomah Falls and along the first mile of (nearly vertical, nicely switchbacked) trail to Larch Mountain and Sherrard Point. Six flows are exposed from the Columbia River to the top of Multnomah Falls. Especially noteworthy is the pillow lava visible near the top of the falls.

Larch Mountain (4,056 feet) is a small Pleistocene shield volcano of the High Cascades that erupted about 1.8 to 1.4 million years ago. Most of its lavas were basalts. It provides a commanding view of the Columbia River and Portland Basin.

Trail Guide: The first mile of the trail is paved with asphalt, photographers, children, dogs, and busloads of tourists. The viewpoints are great places to look at the five Grande Ronde Columbia River basalt flows exposed beneath the combined 620-foot drop of the upper and lower falls.

From Interstate 84 east of Portland, take Multnomah Falls exit 31. (Alternatively, take the Columbia River Scenic Highway exit 28 to Multnomah Falls for a more intimate drive along the gorge.)

Pillow basalts are visible beneath Upper Multnomah Falls.

The trail, USFS 441, begins on the east flank of Multnomah Lodge. Note especially the pillow lavas (lumpy forms) just beneath the upper falls. Continue upward on the trail. It provides an up-close view of a moss-laden, fine-grained Grande Ronde flow. The top of the falls, at 0.9 mile, reveals a grand view of the Columbia River.

From here, the trail climbs along Multnomah Creek at a steady clip. One large falls and many cascades plunge over the Columbia River basalt

Grande Ronde flows along Multnomah Creek. At 4.5 miles into the hike, the slope steepens again as the trail encounters the young basalt of Larch Mountain's shield volcano. This rock is difficult to distinguish from Columbia River basalt. Generally, it is more brittle and lighter colored. Its small crystals are visible if you look very closely.

At almost 7 miles, the trail reaches the picnic and parking area just south of Larch Mountain summit. Another 300 yards to the viewpoint rewards the weary hiker with great views from Sherrard Point.

Hike 16

ROWENA CREST AND TOM McCALL PRESERVE

Faults, Folds, and Scablands

Scablands created by the Ice-Age Missoula floods plus the summit of McCall Point provide views of folding and faulting.

DISTANCE ■ **4 miles**

ELEVATION ■ **700 to 1,722 feet**

DIFFICULTY ■ **Moderate**

TOPOGRAPHIC MAP ■ **Lyle, Wash.**

GEOLOGIC MAPS ■ **1, 21**

PRECAUTIONS ■ **The trails cover a preserve of The Nature Conservancy; picking plants (except non-native, noxious weeds) is forbidden. Hazards may include rattlesnakes, poison oak, and ticks.**

FOR INFORMATION ■ **The Nature Conservancy**

About the Landscape: From the top of Tom McCall Point and from Interstate 84 between Hood River and The Dalles, you can see something strange on the Washington side of the river: the basalt layers are tilted. Worse yet, just where the tilt skies out, there is a crashing big collection of vertical rock spikes called the Ortley Pinnacles. They are composed of broken, angular rocks cemented together. This is a fault zone, a place where the Columbia River basalts have been violently thrust westward, one set of twelve basalt flows riding up and over the others, creating the cobbled, broken rocks of the Ortley Pinnacles. In this part of the Columbia River Gorge, the Columbia River basalts have been gently folded as well as faulted. These folds developed in the basalts from 16 to about 10 million years ago.

On this hike you can also explore the austere landscape left by the Missoula floods, which submerged the overlook at Rowena Crest beneath as much as 200 feet of water. The initial surges of this raging, turbulent water stripped away rock, leaving a barren, knobby topography. Once the high-energy, high-impact floodwaters had slowed, sand and gravel bars were left perched hundreds of feet above the present river. One lies north across the river above the town of Lyle, Washington. Another is still higher on the walls of the Klickitat River valley northwest of Lyle.

Since the floods, the active Mount St. Helens volcano repeatedly blew out clouds of volcanic ash which built up to a thickness of about 3 feet on Rowena Plateau. Subsequent erosion of this ash produced the subdued *biscuit mound* topography you can see all around you.

Trail Guide: A developed overlook is found at Rowena Crest, but there are better views from Tom McCall Point and the Tom McCall Preserve. Two trails—one to the summit and the other across the lower basalt prairie—cover this Nature Conservancy preserve.

From I-84, take Rowena exit 76. Turn south on the Columbia River Scenic Highway, and drive 3.4 miles west, up the curving old highway to Rowena Crest and the parking area.

The trail to the summit of Tom McCall Point departs from the end of the parking area's solid stone fence and heads across a lumpy prairie composed of Mount St. Helens ash deposited atop the basalts. At 0.5 mile into the walk, the trail rounds a large basalt *scab* (a steep-sided rock outcrop) eroded by the Missoula floods and begins a more serious ascent. The trail crosses the Pomona and Priest Rapids flows of the Columbia River basalt, and after a steep climb of steps literally carved into the Priest Rapids flow, emerges atop the gravels that cap Tom McCall Point, 1.5 miles from the up-bound trailhead. This vantage point provides exceptional views downstream and limited views toward The Dalles. Return the way you came.

The lower trail across the relatively flat ash-mantled scabland starts at a turnout on the road near the crest; a sign just inside a wire fence marks the trailhead. This 1-mile round-trip trail provides a scenic tour of several small ponds and wetlands. These wetlands have developed in depressions scoured by the Missoula floods and later filled by ash from Mount St. Helens. You can peer over the edge of a small canyon carved into the basalts, filled by flood sediments, and now being excavated again by the tireless creek. Return the way you came.

Chapter 5.
THE CASCADES

Glacial striations on rimrock, Crater Lake

The Cascade Mountains define and divide Oregon. As the state's ecologic and geologic backbone, they separate desert from rain forest and ancient rocks from young terranes. The Cascades are a community of peaks, each with a separate history, but each an integral part of the whole.

The Cascades are really two mountain ranges in one, two parallel belts of volcanic rocks of different ages. The older, steep-sloped, and heavily forested Western Cascades belt hosts the rumpled and eroded relics of volcanos 45 to about 8 million years in age. Today we think of this eroded, once-mighty volcanic range as merely the Cascade foothills, from Sweet Home to Detroit, or Vida to McKenzie Bridge.

The younger belt of volcanos, erupted during the last 5 million years, is called the High Cascades. The High Cascades mountains include the familiar, photogenic volcanic peaks as well as a thick foundation of lavas

STRATOVOLCANOS AND SHIELD VOLCANOS

When you think of a volcano, the first image that probably comes to mind is a stratovolcano. Mount Hood. Mount St. Helens. Mount Rainier. Mount Fuji. Stratovolcanos, sometimes called composite cones, are the classic peaks built above subduction zones.

Lava and ash eruptions alternate in stratovolcanos. They may erupt almost any composition of lava, from basalt to rhyolite. Most produce basalt early in their history and the more explosive rhyolite as they age. Stratovolcanos thrive on variety: a lava here, a mudflow there, an eruption of cinders, an eruption of ash, one century an andesite, the next a rhyolite. Most eruptions build only a small portion of the cone, rather than covering the entire mountain.

Shield volcanos are far more single-minded than their multilayered cousins. Shield volcanos erupt mostly basalt. Their low-slung profiles may look more like a puddle of cold molasses than a volcano. But shield volcanos are every bit as famous: Mauna Loa, Newberry, and, in the Cascades, Mount Sheridan, just south of Bachelor, are shields. The largest shield volcano in the solar system is Olympus Mons on Mars, with a diameter of 370 miles and a summit elevation of 16 miles.

beneath them. While some High Cascades volcanos can be considered extinct, Mount Hood and South Sister are likely to erupt again.

The older Western Cascades include lavas, mudflows, and tuffs (consolidated ash). Their peaks once rose as high as today's volcanos. But all we have today are their altered and eroded roots.

The Western Cascades erupted in three periods: (1) From 50 to 30 million years ago the Western Cascades built volcanos that may have looked like today's High Cascade Range. (2) From 30 to 15 million years ago ash erupted. The wind-blown ash produced the Painted Hills and buried rhinos and saber-toothed tigers in the John Day Fossil Beds. These eruptions created gold deposits in the upper Santiam River basin. (3) The last volcanic activity of the Western Cascades, from 9 to about 7 million years ago, produced basalt. At the same time, the Western Cascades began to fold gently upward, and may still be gradually rising.

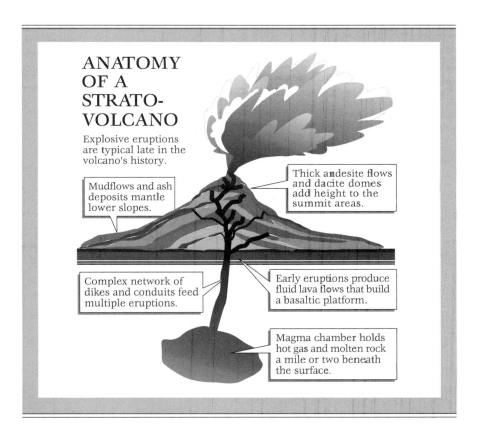

ANATOMY OF A STRATO-VOLCANO

Explosive eruptions are typical late in the volcano's history.

Mudflows and ash deposits mantle lower slopes.

Thick andesite flows and dacite domes add height to the summit areas.

Complex network of dikes and conduits feed multiple eruptions.

Early eruptions produce fluid lava flows that build a basaltic platform.

Magma chamber holds hot gas and molten rock a mile or two beneath the surface.

Mount Hood is a typical stratovolcano.

Oregon's High Cascades, from Crater Lake to Mount Hood, are full-fledged volcanos, and at least two of them (Hood and South Sister) are just biding their time until they erupt again.

The High Cascades also grew in three stages: (1) From 5 to about 2 million years ago, eruptions of basalt built low-lying shield volcanos along today's High Cascade axis. (2) About 2 million years ago, faulting produced a valley (called the High Cascade *graben*) along the Cascade crest. Green Ridge, east of Mount Jefferson, represents the east wall of this graben. Basalt eruptions filled this valley. (3) Beginning a little less than 1 million years ago, during the Ice Age, the modern High Cascade peaks began to erupt. Most of these volcanos were stratovolcanos.

As volcanos grew, glaciers wore them down. The oldest High Cascade peaks are the most eroded by glaciers. Some, including Three Fingered Jack and Mount Washington, have been virtually erased by glaciation. The more vigorous volcanos (Mount Hood, Mount Jefferson, and South Sister) maintained their youthful physique by erupting in defiance of glacial attack.

Glacial striations near Tam McArthur Rim

TABLE ROCK

Hike 17

WESTERN CASCADES AND HIGH CASCADES MEET

Take a close-up view of the Western Cascades' younger rocks and the oldest basalts of the High Cascades.

DISTANCE ▪ 5.2 miles

ELEVATION ▪ 3,625 to 4,880 feet

DIFFICULTY ▪ Moderate

TOPOGRAPHIC MAP ▪ Rooster Rock

GEOLOGIC MAP ▪ 1

PRECAUTIONS ▪ Beware of cliffs at the summit!

FOR INFORMATION ▪ Salem Bureau of Land Management office

About the Landscape: Table Rock and Rooster Rock rise above the Mollalla River drainage. This dual-summited plateau is composed of two ages of rocks. The base of Table Mountain is formed of 17- to 10-million-year-old andesites. These rocks probably once were part of a stratovolcano between Estacada and Mill City. Today they appear only in a few roadcuts and stream banks.

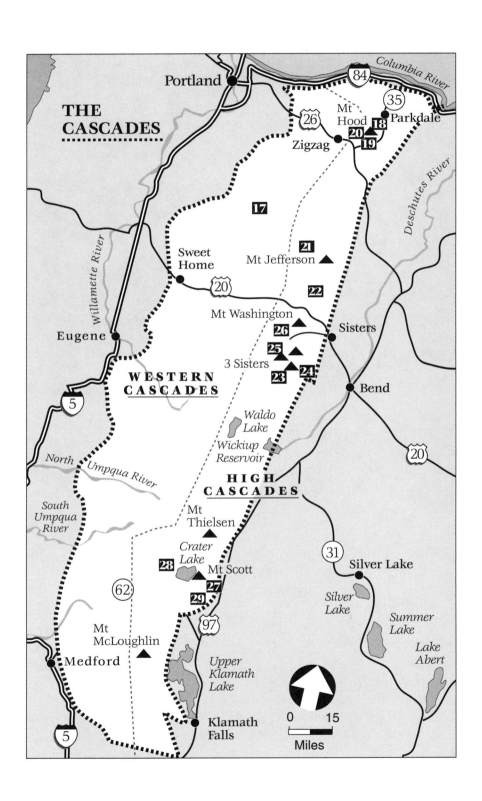

THE
CASCADES

Portland

Columbia River

84

35

Mt
Hood

18

Parkdale

26

20

Zigzag

19

Deschutes River

17

21

Mt Jefferson

Sweet
Home

20

22

Mt Washington

26

Sisters

Eugene

25

WESTERN
CASCADES

3 Sisters

24

23

Bend

5

Waldo
Lake

Wickiup
Reservoir

20

North

Umpqua River

HIGH
CASCADES

South
Umpqua
River

Mt
Thielsen

Crater
Lake

28

Mt Scott

31

Silver Lake

62

27

Silver
Lake

Summer
Lake

29

Mt
McLoughlin

97

Lake
Abert

Medford

Upper
Klamath
Lake

5

Klamath
Falls

0   15

Miles

Willamette River

Basalt forms the summit of Table Mountain and Rooster Rock. It may be associated with the High Cascades. Its age is about 4 million years.

Trail Guide: This is a short, steep hike to the summit of Table Rock. Nearby Rooster Rock can be reached by an optional 1.7-mile (one way) side trip.

From Oregon Highway 211 in Mollala, turn south on South Mathias Road, then left on South Feyrer Park Road. About 1.7 miles up this road, cross the Mollala River bridge and turn right on South Dickey Prairie Road. In 5.3 miles cross the river again, then bear left on South Mollala Road, remaining on pavement. After almost 13 miles, bear left on gravel Middle Fork Road. Then in 2.6 miles, turn right onto Table Rock Road. From this junction drive 5.8 miles to the poorly marked trailhead on the right side of the road.

The trail penetrates a forest of large Douglas-fir and substantial understory as it climbs toward the broad summit. This vegetation obscures the older Western Cascades that form the base of Table and Rooster Rocks. At 1.2 miles the trail emerges from the forest and navigates a talus slope at the base of a 150-foot-high cliff of columnar basalt. This is the younger basalt that forms the summit of Table and Rooster Rocks. The well-developed columns and thickness of the flow suggest it is a basalt flow from one of the early High Cascades shield volcanos that flowed down a canyon of the ancestral Mollala River about 4 million years ago.

At 2.1 miles the trail reaches a saddle and a junction. Turn left for the 0.5-mile hike north to the top of Table Rock. (For the optional side trip to Rooster Rock, turn right.) From the top of Table Rock, an outcrop of relatively old High Cascades basalt, there are picture-perfect views of Mount Hood, Mount Jefferson, and the wrinkled Western Cascades.

MOUNT HOOD

Oregon's highest peak is also the one most likely to erupt again. Mount Hood's last major eruption occurred about 1790. The twisted stumps of whitebark pine executed by its force still lie in state above Mount Hood Meadows.

At least three volcanos have occupied the area where Mount Hood rises today. The first, which produced rocks called the Rhododendron Formation, appeared about 8 million years ago. Its lavas form Zigzag and Tom, Dick, and Harry Mountains. The second, Sandy Glacier volcano, was active about 1.4 million years ago. Today it is tucked into the south flanks of Mount Hood. The third is Mount Hood itself.

The mountain we know as Mount Hood began its life about 730,000 years ago. Thick andesite lavas built its main cone. But by 29,000 years ago, lava eruptions dwindled. The only exception is the Parkdale flow, a

6,000-year-old basalt sequestered in apple and pear orchards about 2 miles west of Parkdale.

Since the Ice Age, four periods of eruptions have shaken Mount Hood. The last eruptive episode (the Old Maid period) occurred about the year 1790. These eruptions vented at Crater Rock. They produced steam, ash, and a small, three-lobed dacite dome which is Crater Rock itself. The eruption melted snow and glacial ice, unleashing enormous mudflows that buried the forest on Old Maid Flat. We may still be living in the Old Maid period today.

In the last half century, Mount Hood's volcanic activity has killed two people. In 1934 a climber exploring the ice caves in Coalman Glacier was suffocated by the oxygen-poor gas emitted from the Crater Rock fumaroles. In 1980 a debris flow on Pollalie Creek spawned by rapid glacial melting killed one person and wiped out a 5-mile section of Highway 35. Even without erupting, Mount Hood remains a volcanic force to be reckoned with.

Hike
18

SANDY GLACIER VOLCANO

Mount Hood's Ancestor

View the 1.2-million-year-old Sandy Glacier volcano, which protrudes from Hood's west flank just below Sandy Glacier.

DISTANCE ■ 10.2 miles

ELEVATION ■ 3,000 to 6,285 feet

DIFFICULTY ■ Strenuous

TOPOGRAPHIC MAPS ■ Mount Hood South, Mount Hood North

GEOLOGIC MAPS ■ 22–24

PRECAUTIONS ■ The spur road 1825-100 to the trailhead is rough; 4WD or high-clearance vehicle is recommended.

FOR INFORMATION ■ Zigzag Ranger District

About the Landscape: The relict of the Sandy Glacier volcano protrudes from the west slopes of Mount Hood like a joey peeking from mother kangaroo's pouch. The Sandy Glacier volcano's vent area is exposed as dark orange-brown rocks hidden in the head of the Muddy Creek and Sandy River canyons. Like Hood, the Sandy Glacier volcano was a stratovolcano. Unlike Hood, which has erupted mostly andesite, the Sandy Glacier volcano erupted mostly basalt.

GEOLOGIC TIMETABLE 5: THE CASCADES

Five significant events that shaped the landscape

Millions of years ago	Geologic era	Geologic event
0.0002 (the year 1790)	Holocene	Last major eruptions of Mount Hood, the Old Maid period; mudflows and explosive ash-flow tuffs
0.007	Holocene	Cataclysmic eruption of Mount Mazama
0.730	Pleistocene	First eruptions of vents that will build to High Cascade peaks
5–0.730	Pliocene to Pleistocene	Early eruptions of High Cascade shield volcanos and calderas
40–10	Oligocene to Miocene	Western Cascades volcanos erupt

The crags near Mount Hood's summit are easily visible on this hike. They provide proof of Hood's volcanic virility. At Hot Rocks near Hood's summit, boiling water and sulfur-laden gas still escape. Crater Rock, the large knob above Timberline Lodge, is a dacite dome, site of the last major Hood eruption in the 1790s.

Trail Guide: This rigorous hike takes you from Ramona Falls, which tumbles over a broad face of hard basalt with well-developed columns (these rocks form the base of Mount Hood's cone, and probably date to 500,000 to 700,000 years), to the base of the Sandy Glacier volcano via the Pacific Crest Trail and a scramble up Muddy Fork of the Sandy River.

To reach the trailhead, from Zigzag on US 26 take USFS Road 18 north about 4.5 miles past Riley campground, to USFS Road 1825. Drive about 1.8 miles, then take spur road 1825-100 (trail 770) to the Ramona Falls (trail 797) trailhead.

Trail 797 splits, one leg going up the east side of the canyon, the other the west. Take one going up and return along the other. Both explore the stunted forest growing on the Old Maid mudflow of 1790. The trails meet at the base of Ramona Falls, 2.1 miles into the hike.

At Ramona Falls, the hike joins the Timberline and Pacific Crest trails. The PCT rises up Yocum Ridge through fern-draped forest to the junction with the Yocum Ridge Trail in 0.6 mile. For the best view of Sandy Glacier volcano, continue on the PCT rather than taking the Yocum Ridge spur trail. The PCT ambles through forest for 2.4 miles, reaching the Muddy Fork at a clearing that permits an outstanding view of the exhumed remnants of the Sandy Glacier volcano as well as the younger vents near Mount Hood's summit. A 1-mile, slow hike up the Muddy Fork and a scrambling climb over talus brings you to the basalt outcrops at the base of Sandy Glacier volcano.

The return route retraces the path along Muddy Fork and the PCT (also called Timberline Trail here) to Ramona Falls. From here, return to the trailhead on the path you didn't hike in on.

TIMBERLINE TRAIL

Hike 19

CLOUD CAP TO TIMBERLINE LODGE

Explore the andesites of Mount Hood and the ghost forests created by Mount Hood's eruption in the 1790s.

DISTANCE ■ 13 miles one way

ELEVATION ■ 4,900 to 8,600 feet

DIFFICULTY ■ Moderate to strenuous

TOPOGRAPHIC MAPS ■ Mount Hood South, Mount Hood North

GEOLOGIC MAPS ■ 22–24

PRECAUTIONS ■ This hike requires a shuttle vehicle at Timberline Lodge. Because of its length, it's best done as an overnight backpack.

FOR INFORMATION ■ Hood River Ranger District

About the Landscape: One of the most provocative places on Mount Hood lies a mile above Mount Hood Meadows. On this ridge east of the White River, skeletal stumps of whitebark pine convey the agony of their deaths in Mount Hood's 1790s eruption. Like the trees felled more recently by Mount St. Helens, these aged stumps lie parallel, tops pointed away from the mountain's violent blast, weatherbeaten roots grasping only air. This most recent eruption of Mount Hood emanated from Crater Rock, a stubby pinnacle—geologically a dacite plug dome—on the south side of Hood's summit. The force that felled this forest was a hot, dense ash cloud, with temperatures above 700 degrees Centigrade (about 1,250 degrees Fahrenheit). Based on the size and form of the trees it felled, its speed has been calculated at 84 mph.

A related ghost forest of fir and pine, now emerging as jagged stumps, is buried in the ash and mudflows of White River canyon.

On the northeast slopes of Mount Hood, Cooper Spur provides an unforgettable view of Eliot Glacier. Eliot is the largest glacier in Oregon. From Cooper Spur you can study the crevasse system and, on a hot August day, listen to the ice groan and crack.

Trail Guide: Travel the Timberline Trail and a bit of the Pacific Crest Trail from Cloud Cap to Timberline, with a backcountry overnight near the head

Bleached stumps of trees killed in Mount Hood's last major eruption in the 1790s

of Mitchell Creek or on the southeast slopes of Gnarl Ridge. Leave a shuttle vehicle at Timberline Lodge before continuing to the Cloud Cap trailhead.

To reach the Cloud Cap trailhead, on Highway 35 14 miles south of Hood River, take the Parkdale exit. At an intersection marked by a blinking light just east of Parkdale, continue straight on Cooper Spur Road, which becomes USFS Road 3512 and reaches the trailhead in about 24 miles. The rocky outcrops at the campground are andesite, and they provide a first-class view of Mount Hood, Eliot Glacier, Langrille Glacier, and Langrille Crags—the shattered relics of andesite flows.

Take the Timberline Trail south toward Timberline Lodge, heading straight out of the small campground at Cloud Cap through a forest and nicely banded rhyodacite boulders, and skirting the east *moraine* of Eliot

Jointed andesites near the Cloud Cap trailhead curve skyward in the direction of their last movement.

Glacier before climbing through a small forest of stunted lodgepole to the Cooper Spur trail, 1 mile from the trailhead.

The Cooper Spur trail turns west from the Timberline Trail and climbs steadily across *pumice* and moraine for about 2.3 miles. In early summer, be prepared to cross extensive snowfields on your way up this ridge. The hikers' trail ends at the edge of Newton Clark Glacier's snowfield at about 8,600 feet. This windy vantage point provides a tutorial in the complexity of glacial crevasses—and the complexity of glacial noises. The Chimney, a horned crag of dacite and *pyroclastic rocks* (fragmented rock explosively ejected by a volcano) near Hood's east summit, hovers above. Hood's summit rocks are crumbly and seamed with yellow. They have been altered by steam and sulfur-rich gas over thousands of years. Return the 2.3 miles to the Timberline Trail and rejoin it to continue south and west.

From its junction with the Cooper Spur trail, the highest part of Timberline Trail crosses a treeless plain of pumice and glacial outwash. It crosses several snowfields, rounds Lambertson Butte, teeters along the brink of Gnarl Ridge and Newton Creek, and dives into Newton Creek's layered canyon, 3.6 miles from the Cooper Spur trail junction.

On the west side of the Newton Creek canyon, Timberline Trail crosses rugged and more forested terrain. Good campsites can be found in the headwaters of Heather Canyon, 7.5 miles from Cloud Cap campground. The Timberline Trail ducks beneath the ski lifts of Mount Hood Meadows Ski Area before crossing a Mount Hood Meadows access road and intersecting the Umbrella Falls trail (trail 667), where more campsites can be found at 8.9 miles from Cloud Cap.

The forest of whitebark pine killed in the 1790s eruption of Mount Hood lies off the Timberline Trail about 0.5 mile above (north of) the Umbrella Falls trail intersection, at elevations above 7,000 feet. Walk across open slopes to these trees, which make Hood's eruptive potential seem very, very real.

Continuing on to Timberline Lodge, now only 4 miles away, the trail crosses the White River canyon. This river is treacherous to cross in the spring and early to midsummer. The White River carves its steep and unstable canyon through ash and mudflows. The layers in the canyon wall are layers of ash, cinders, and mudflows unleashed by the pulses of eruptions two centuries ago. The river is excavating a forest of twisted Douglas-fir stumps, buried by an eruption from a layer near the canyon bottom. These trees can be viewed from the Lost Forest overlook area.

It is an easy 0.6 mile from the west edge of the White River canyon to Timberline Lodge, where the Timberline and Pacific Crest trails coincide.

LOST CREEK NATURE TRAIL

Hike 20

THE OLD MAID ERUPTION

Explore the Old Maid mudflows of the most recent eruption of Mount Hood and a Lost Forest exhumed along Lost Creek.

DISTANCE ■ 0.5-mile loop

ELEVATION ■ 2,310 to 2,320 feet

DIFFICULTY ■ Easy

TOPOGRAPHIC MAPS ■ Government Camp, Bull Run Lake

GEOLOGIC MAPS ■ 22–24

PRECAUTIONS ■ None

FOR INFORMATION ■ Zigzag Ranger District

About the Landscape: In the middle of Lost Creek, where it borders the trail as well as farther down, rise huge, jagged-topped stumps. In an old-growth forest where large trees and stumps are normal, this situation at first appears quite ordinary—except that trees don't usually grow in the middle of streams.

These stumps are all that remain of trees buried by mudflows during Mount Hood's 1790s eruption (the hot, viscous mud prevented the stumps from rotting). The tops of many of these "very old"-growth trees have been snapped off, suggesting that, like the 1980 eruption of Mount St. Helens, the 1790s eruption of Mount Hood produced explosive blasts as well as speedy mudflows.

Trail Guide: From US 26 at Zigzag, turn north onto Lolo Pass Road (USFS Road 18) and continue 4 miles. Turn east on USFS Road 1825. Lost Creek Picnic Area and the trail are 2.2 miles along USFS Road 1825.

This self-guided, handicapped-accessible trail leads through an old-growth forest stand of cedar and Douglas-fir that was largely spared from catastrophic forest fires of 1893 and 1906. The paved trail passes signed interpretive sites about beaver ponds, wetlands, and forests before threading its way back to the parking lot.

MOUNT JEFFERSON

Mount Jefferson rises to 10,495 feet, dominating the Santiam and Metolius skylines. But Oregon's second-highest peak is just a shadow of its former self. The mountain may have topped 12,000 feet before glaciers chiseled it into submission.

Jefferson is a large pile of andesites built on a foundation of basalt. The oldest rocks around Mount Jefferson are 6.5- to 3.9-million-year-old basalts and andesites. They compose Devils Hill and line the canyons of the North

Lost Creek exhumes a tree buried by a mudflow from the 1790s eruption of Mount Hood.

Santiam and Breitenbush Rivers. About 2.5 million years ago a large shield volcano was centered at Hole in the Wall. The remnants of this cone form Bear Butte.

The lavas that would form Mount Jefferson's high cone began erupting about 680,000 years ago. These first eruptions produced basalt. Then, about 350,000 years ago, Mount Jefferson underwent a volcanic midlife crisis. Instead of basalt, it began to erupt andesite and dacite from vents such as Goat Peak on the mountain's south flank.

Although Mount Jefferson has not erupted in at least the last 15,000 years, volcanic activity near the mountain is more recent. Forked Butte, a cinder cone about 5 miles south of Jefferson's summit, produced basalt lava flows about 6,500 years ago. The existence of hot springs such as Breitenbush suggest that the magma chambers below Jefferson may still be warm.

CARL LAKE TO HOLE IN THE WALL

Hike 21

Mount Jefferson's History

Examine andesites and Forked Butte and descend to Hole in the Wall, a volcanic vent exposed in a glacial cirque.

DISTANCE ■ **17 miles one way**

ELEVATION ■ **3,040 to 5,903 feet**

DIFFICULTY ■ **Strenuous**

TOPOGRAPHIC MAPS ■ **Mount Jefferson, Lionshead, Marion Lake, Candle Creek**

GEOLOGIC MAPS ■ **25, 26**

PRECAUTIONS ■ **This hike requires a shuttle vehicle at the Jefferson Lake trailhead. Because of the hike's length, camp overnight at either Carl Lake or Table Lake and day-hike to Hole in the Wall.**

FOR INFORMATION ■ **Sisters Ranger District**

About the Landscape: Most of what we can see of Mount Jefferson today is andesite. Older basalts, including the rocks of Bear Butte, and the very young (6,500 years) basalts of Forked Butte give variety to the gray landscape of Jefferson. Plenty of glacially polished bedrock and glacially sculpted lakes attest to the power of ice here. Most of the hike's route explores the andesites that once formed the flanks of Jefferson's original and much larger cone.

The view of Jefferson from near Table Rock and Forked Butte showcases Goat Rock—the vent area for andesite eruptions of Jefferson 350,000 years ago—which appears as a knob three-quarters of the way to the summit on the mountain's south face. The plug at the top of the mountain is not a central vent at all, but an eroded andesite lava flow.

Trail Guide: This long hike begins at the Cabot Lake trailhead and ends at the Jefferson Lake trailhead and is best planned with at least one overnight at Carl Lake or Table Lake. Day hike to Hole in the Wall from Carl or

Mount Jefferson is a mostly andesite volcano that has been extensively eroded by glaciers.

Table Lake for a lengthier and more leisurely exploration of the area.

To reach the Cabot Lake trailhead, on US 20 approximately 11 miles west of Sisters, turn north onto USFS Road 12. In 3.5 miles, turn left (west) onto Road 1230 and follow it 12 miles to the Cabot Lake trailhead (trail 4003). To drop a shuttle vehicle at the destination trailhead, from Cabot Lake trailhead take USFS Road 1280 4 miles back to USFS Road 12, then turn west on USFS Road 1290 for 1 mile and follow USFS Road 1292 for 2 miles.

The trail to Cabot Lake and Mount Jefferson (trail 4003) rises straight and slowly through a forest of Douglas-fir, western white pine, lodgepole pine, and white fir. Through the trees, the trail allows glimpses of the rugged, dark basalt flow that emanated from Forked Butte in the valley bottom. A mile to the north is Sugar Pine ridge, a 2.5-million-year-old shield volcano.

The trail switchbacks past First and Second Ponds, to reach Third Pond in 2 miles. These three small lakes are *glacial kettles,* formed when ice buried in a glacial moraine melts. They now provide welcome wetlands. First Pond is peppered with dark, rounded basalt boulders probably quarried by glaciers from the basalt shield that underlies North Cinder Peak. The trail continues from this wetlands area on an easy grade for another mile to Carl Lake at 5,480 feet. The outcrops here have been smoothed by glaciers, making this a good spot to camp.

The trail from Carl Lake heads north, climbing the steep front of several andesite flows and crossing a flat tableland containing several small, shallow lakes, including Junction Lake, 2.2 miles north along the trail. From Junction Lake, the trail traverses glacially scoured bedrock and passes the dark, rubbly basalt flows from Forked Butte. These 6,500-year-old *aa* flows (a Hawaiian term for lavas that cool like crumb-cakes, with broken or fractured pieces of the flow on their surface) are the youngest eruptions in the Mount Jefferson area.

From the rocky plateau just north of Forked Butte, Jefferson looms ahead, with Bear Butte to its east. Table Rock frames the west side of this small plateau. The trail drops from the andesite plateau to dark, forest-swaddled Patsy Lake, and the junction with the Jefferson Lake trail, 1.9 miles north of Junction Lake.

Continue north on trail 4003 to Table Lake. This large, glacially carved lake provides good camping sites. From Table Lake, continue on trail 4003 for 2.5 miles to Hole in the Wall. Trail 4003 ambles up the west flank of Bear Butte. At the ridge crest, the slope plunges abruptly into Hole in the Wall. This glacial cirque exposes the vent complex for the 2.5-million-year-old Bear Butte volcano. The trail switchbacks into and dead-ends in this cirque which serves as headwaters of Jefferson Creek.

From Hole in the Wall, return 2.5 miles to Table Lake. On the next day, retrace the trail from Table Lake 1 mile to Patsy Lake and the junction with the Jefferson Lake trail. Head east along the Jefferson Lake trail, which is intertwined with the rugged 6,500-year-old basalt flows of Forked Butte. The trail winds across the lava flows, and invites refreshing stops at Lava Spring and Cougar Spring. Old-growth pines and Douglas-fir more than 6 feet in diameter greet the weary hiker 10 miles from Table Lake downslope near the trailhead.

THREE FINGERED JACK

Three Fingered Jack's jaggedy, raggedy silhouette rises between Mount Jefferson and the Three Sisters. It is a mountain with racing stripes, a spectacular layered and dissected volcanic biography, a slice through time. Nowhere—not at Crater Lake or Broken Top or the bare and crumbling slopes of Mount Theilsen—is a full-scale cross section of a stratovolcano better exposed.

Three Fingered Jack began its life about 300,000 years ago as a small cinder cone. The remnants of this cone appear as the orange, red, and gray layers in the west-facing wall of the present mountain.

The second eruptive episode of Three Fingered Jack occurred about 250,000 years ago. The mountain built a more massive cone 0.25 mile west of the first cone. Lava flows alternated with cinders, scoria, lava bombs, and other unconsolidated material. At its apex, Three Fingered Jack rose to an elevation of perhaps 9,000 feet.

In its last major eruptions, perhaps 200,000 years ago, the vent of Three Fingered Jack shifted to a position near the north edge of the existing peak. This new basalt magma solidified as a broad intrusive plug that buttresses the northern flank of the mountain.

Three major glacial periods have affected Three Fingered Jack. They carved away the entire north side of the quiet, dying volcano. Three Fingered Jack, unlike Mount Hood, Jefferson, and Three Sisters, could not produce enough volume to replace what glaciers had carved away. The peak we see today is only a skeletal relict of the southern flank of a major stratovolcano.

CANYON CREEK TRAIL

ANATOMY OF A STRATOVOLCANO

View the layers of ash and lava that compose a stratovolcano.

Hike 22

DISTANCE ■ 4.3-mile loop
ELEVATION ■ 5,130 to 6,500 feet
DIFFICULTY ■ Moderate
TOPOGRAPHIC MAP ■ Three Fingered Jack
GEOLOGIC MAP ■ 25
PRECAUTIONS ■ None
FOR INFORMATION ■ Sisters Ranger District

About the Landscape: From the top of its fresh moraine, Three Fingered Jack provides a lesson in stratovolcano history. Red bands generally are scoria—rust red, iron-rich oxidized cinders coughed from a volcanic throat. Yellow bands are better-consolidated, finer-grained material, mostly ash and tuff. A few ignimbrites or ash-flow tuffs, yellow to buff in color, provide variety. A major conduit of very fine-grained diorite forms the dark core of Three Fingered Jack. Angular chunks of this rock litter the moraine. There is evidence in these cliffs for multiple eruptive cycles. Dikes carrying fresh lava cross-cut the ash-and-lava layer cake. Troughs indicate old stream channels filled with pumice. The wall east of this moraine shows similar features that developed earlier in the volcano's history.

Trail Guide: This hike investigates Three Fingered Jack via the Canyon Creek trail. To optimize the view of Three Fingered Jack's colorful east face, plan this as an early morning hike, leaving the trailhead just after dawn. Or arrange an overnight stay in Canyon Creek Meadow and view the mountain in the morning.

To reach the trailhead, from US Highway 20 about 12 miles west of Sisters, take USFS Road 12 north 3.5 miles to USFS Road 1230, drive 2 miles

Three Fingered Jack rises above the Canyon Creek trail.

on USFS Road 1230 to USFS Road 1234, and turn onto USFS Road 1234 and drive about 6 miles to Jack Lake and the Canyon Creek trailhead.

The Canyon Creek trail begins on the north side of the parking area, skirts the east shore of Jack Lake, and then lines out on a westward track. From the meadows above Jack Lake the jagged summit of Three Fingered Jack looms ahead. Three Fingered Jack's yellow, red, and gray banding represent ash, cinders, and lava from the eruptions that built the volcano.

At the junction with the Wasco Lake trail, 0.3 mile into the hike, turn left and continue on the Canyon Creek trail (trail 4010). The Canyon Creek trail rises across glacial gravels and crosses andesite outcrops of the oldest Three Fingered Jack eruptions, scoots past two shallow lakes that represent *glacial kettles* (lakes in shallow depressions left by a chunk of glacial ice), and crests in about 1 mile at the entrance to a dense fir forest.

From the crest, the Canyon Creek trail plunges through a moss-festooned stand of true fir. At the bottom, it emerges into a series of clearings, turns south, and crosses multiple gravelly moraines and areas of glacial outwash. In another mile, the trail leads to the last moraine built by Three Finger Jack's voracious glaciers. The moraine contains a variety of rocks from the now-erased mountain. Informal paths stretch to the top. A view of a calm, milky turquoise lake, a classic tarn of *glacial milchwasser* (German for "milk-water," so named because of the milky or cloudy appearance that suspended clays impart to water) rewards the effort required to climb the gravel hill. From the top of the moraine, a narrow path teeters about 200 yards toward the east face of Three Fingered Jack for a closer view of the diorite plug.

To return to the trailhead, retrace the Canyon Creek trail 4010 about 2.5 miles to its intersection with the Wasco Lake trail, and follow this trail uphill back to the trailhead.

THREE SISTERS AREA

The central Cascades are the most popular and accessible portion of the High Cascades. They are also the most geologically complex. Although eruption of the Three Sisters area began about 5 million years ago, the peaks we see today were all built during the last third of the Pleistocene. The oldest—and most glacially eroded—volcanos of the Three Sisters area include The Wife, The Husband, Black Crater, and Broken Top.

North Sister began its eruptions 300,000 years ago. It started as a small shield volcano, then built a larger cinder cone, and finally produced lava and dikes to form today's peak. Collier Cone, a basaltic cinder cone just north of the mountain, is among the youngest (less than 5,000 years old) eruptive centers in the High Cascades.

Middle Sister, partly submerged in glacial ice and partly carried away by it, is the least accessible and least distinctive—and the most complex—of the Three Sisters. It could never decide which of its siblings it wanted to mimic, so it erupted both basalt, like North Sister, and andesite, like South Sister.

South Sister began erupting andesite and dacite more than 200,000 years ago. At the end of the Pleistocene, it constructed cinder cones on its summit. Nearby, LeConte and Cayuse Cones erupted less than 9,500 years ago. Rock Mesa and Devils Chain are less than 2,000 years old. South Sister rests uneasily and retains the potential to erupt.

Mount Bachelor is the youngest major volcano in the Three Sisters area. It is less than 15,000 years old. Mount Bachelor began as a flat shield volcano, then shifted to erupt cinders. Egan Cone, on the west side of Mount Bachelor, is the youngest part of the mountain. It erupted between 8,500 and 7,000 years ago. Lavas from Egan Cone are among the most extensive flows from Mount Bachelor. They form the youngest of the multiple lava dams of Sparks Lake.

SOUTH SISTER

SUMMIT AND YOUNGEST VENTS

Explore this stratovolcano, Le Conte Crater, and Rock Mesa, as well as the pumice desert of Wickiup Plain.

DISTANCE ■ 12.6 miles

ELEVATION ■ 5,446 to 10,358 feet

DIFFICULTY ■ Strenuous

TOPOGRAPHIC MAP ■ South Sister

GEOLOGIC MAPS ■ 27, 28

PRECAUTIONS ■ Although no technical skill is required for the climb to South Sister's summit, the last mile is arduous; allow time. Also be aware that weather changes abruptly on the mountain. A permit may be required to camp at Moraine Lake.

FOR INFORMATION ■ Bend Ranger District, Sisters Ranger District

About the Landscape: The closer one approaches South Sister, the more apparent it becomes that this, like all stratovolcanos, is not a simple cone. South Sister is a jumble of domes, andesite flows, feeder dikes, and cinder cones that looks like it was assembled by a committee. Glaciers have quarried away the older, softer rocks, with the exception of the dual summit cinder cones. But they were erupted after glaciers ceased to be a serious threat 8,000 or 9,000 years ago.

The rough-coated rocky features on South Sister's east and west flanks represent the youngest eruptions in this area. Rock Mesa to the west and Devils Hill to the east are dated between 1,800 and 2,600 years. The pumice that veneers the landscape around South Sister and Broken Top came from the eruption of these domes, which are composed of a type of rhyolite. This viscous lava cools quickly, creating the glassy rock called *obsidian*. Le Conte Crater to the west and Cayuse Crater to the east are basalt cinder cones about 6,000 to 10,000 years old. Both erupted basalt lavas from their base.

Trail Guide: This hike follows the Climbers Summit Trail to the upper cinder cone of South Sister, then descends to take a spur trip to Le Conte Crater, Rock Mesa, and Wickiup Plain.

To reach the trailhead, from Bend take the Cascades Lakes Highway (Century Drive) west 25 miles to Sparks Lake. Continue 3 miles west of Sparks Lake, where the Devils Lake Campground turnoff appears on the left. At the north end of the parking area for Devils Lake Campground, the trailhead is marked SOUTH SISTER/MORAINE LAKE/CLIMBERS SUMMIT TRAIL.

The Moraine Lake/Climbers Summit Trail leads through a wetland area, crosses the Cascades Highway, and rises through a moss-festooned forest. At about 1.75 miles, the trail climbs steeply and exits the forest, permitting views of South Sister, Broken Top, and the Devils Hill chain of domes to the east. Just beyond the crest, at about 2 miles, the trail intersects the trail to Wickiup Plain and Le Conte Crater (to the west); stay on the Moraine Lake Climbers Summit Trail. At the next trail junction in 0.3 mile, the Moraine Lake trail parts company with the Climbers Summit Trail; continue north on the unmarked Climbers Summit Trail.

(The Moraine Lake trail shortly begins a descent to Moraine Lake, a good spot for an overnight camp if you wish to make a day-long, leisurely ascent of South Sister.)

Continue north on the Climbers Summit Trail. You can view Rock Mesa and Le Conte Crater by exploring along the west edge of this andesite plateau. The trail continues north for an easy 1.1-mile walk to the base of the South Sister cone. The trail is paved with pumice erupted from Rock Mesa and Devils Hill domes. As you approach South Sister and the Rock Mesa vent to the northwest, this pumice deposit thickens, forming hummocks that resemble low sand dunes.

From the base of the cone to the top, the trail rises 3,600 feet in about 2 miles. At the base of South Sister the trail winds through a gray, platy-jointed andesite flow, then climbs 200 steep feet to glassy outcrops of flow-

Rock Mesa was produced by one of South Sister's most recent eruptions, about 1,800 years ago.

banded rock. The rock glistens like gray obsidian. It is part of a young dome—a blister of thick lava that never developed into a flow. The rounded gray or pinkish globs and some of the holes in this rock are frozen gas bubbles.

Above the *rhyodacite* flow at an elevation of 7,200 feet, the trail clambers over glacially polished rhyodacite and crawls around a wall of rock. This outcrop is part of a large andesite vent system on the volcano's south flank. In the cliff to the east of the trail, columnar joints at the bottom swirl into platy joints at the top, preserving the downslope direction the erupting lava flow.

Above this vent system, the trail traverses the upper cinder cone of South Sister. The hiking is slow due to the looseness of the cinders and the steepness of the trail. The hike to the summit (10,358 feet) skirts Lewis Glacier and edges around South Sister's summit crater. From the top, you can enjoy exceptional views of the adjacent peaks. Chambers Lakes, glacial tarns in small valleys on the north side of the mountain, are especially scenic. Teardrop Pool, in the summit crater, is Oregon's highest lake.

When you've finished soaking up the view, return to the junction of the Climbers Summit Trail with the Moraine Lake/Wickiup Plain trail. Turn west toward Le Conte Crater and Wickiup Plain. This trail leads one mile to Wickiup Plain. A half-mile stroll across the "pumice desert" brings you to the youngest volcanic features of South Sister: Le Conte Crater, a cinder cone about 2,500 years old, and Rock Mesa, a rhyodacite dome and stubby flow about 1,800 years old.

At the base of the Rock Mesa flow, an informal path fades in and out around the perimeter, providing close-up views of all the small-scale features of glassy volcanic rocks. The better trail leads 1.2 miles to the top of Rock Mesa and provides a great view of the ponderous flow patterns now frozen in stone. From Rock Mesa an easy 0.5-mile walk leads across the pumice "desert" of Wickiup Plain to Le Conte Crater. A frozen basalt flow leaks from the base of this 2,500-year-old cinder cone.

Retrace your steps about 2 miles from Wickiup Plain to the trail junction with the Climbers Summit Trail; follow the Climbers Summit Trail 2 miles back to the trailhead.

BROKEN TOP

TODD LAKE TO CRATER CREEK

The anatomy of a stratovolcano is magnificently displayed in the ragged maw of Broken Top.

DISTANCE ■ 7.1 miles

ELEVATION ■ 5,490 to 7,900 feet

DIFFICULTY ■ Moderate

TOPOGRAPHIC MAPS ■ Broken Top, Bachelor Butte

GEOLOGIC MAPS ■ 27–29

PRECAUTIONS ■ A permit may be required to camp at Green Lakes.

FOR INFORMATION ■ Bend Ranger District

About the Landscape: The gray rocks enfolding Todd Lake, where this hike begins, are the remnant of Todd Lake volcano. Todd Lake volcano is much older than the Three Sisters and Broken Top, and has been virtually erased by glaciers.

Broken Top provides an intimate view of stratovolcano anatomy. Despite its exploded appearance, this cone was ravaged by glaciers, not a

Broken Top's ragged profile was carved not by violent eruptions but by glaciers.

cataclysmic eruption. The ragged spires on the northwest are remnants of Broken Top's central volcanic conduit. The layers are alternating ash, lavas, and cinders, each representing a different eruption. The layers thicken, thin, and feather into one another.

Tiny Crook Glacier, cradled in Broken Top's east face, hides behind its imposing moraine like the shriveled Wizard of Oz behind his gilded curtain. Today, the moraine is far more impressive than the withered glacier that built it. The moraine dates to the Little Ice Age in the late seventeenth century. In 1966 glacial meltwater breached the moraine, creating a flood on Crater Creek and carving a wide notch in the moraine's summit.

Trail Guide: From the trailhead at Todd Lake Campground follow the Todd Lake trail to the Broken Top–Green Lakes trail, then take the Broken Top trail to Crater Creek. From here either retrace your route or take a couple of side trips to Crook Glacier and the north side of Broken Top.

To reach the Todd Lake Campground trailhead from Cascade Lakes Highway, turn north at the entrance to the Todd Lake Campground, a gravel road 2 miles west of the Mount Bachelor Ski Area entrance to Todd Lake Campground. Drive approximately 0.5 mile to the parking area for the walk-in campground. The Todd Lake trail begins at the campground entrance.

From Todd Lake, the trail leads upslope at an even grade, crossing light-colored rhyodacite and topping out after about 1.2 miles. A mantle of pumice from Mount Mazama and the eruptions of Rock Mesa and the Devils Hill chain of flows and domes covers the ground. The trail offers several enticing previews of Broken Top as it weaves up and down through forests, alpine meadows, and dry pumice flats.

Follow the signs for Soda Springs Trail, which you intersect in about 2.5 miles. Then continue straight (west) on the trail to Broken Top and Green Lakes, crossing Soda Creek and Crater Creek. At the junction in 1.3 miles,

Crook Glacier, on Broken Top's east face, has nearly disappeared.

111

where the Green Lakes trail leaves the Broken Top trail, turn north onto the Broken Top trail.

The trail continues for about 0.8 mile to the crossing of Crater Creek. Broken Top beckons hikers from the trail. A 0.5-mile walk along Crater Creek brings an intimate view of the devastated volcano and the boulder-strewn recessional moraine of Crook Glacier. An informal trail leads up the moraine.

Return from Crook Glacier to the Broken Top trail, where you continue north to the north side of Broken Top in a 0.8-mile walk. Here you will find the Bend Glacier and more elegantly exposed layers, cross-cut by feeder dikes. Return as you came.

For a short side trip on your return, when you reach the junction of the Broken Top and Green Lakes trails, turn right (west) on the Green Lakes trail for 1 mile to get a close-up view of Cayuse Crater. The trail takes you across the side of Cayuse Crater, just above the vent for basalt flows. This large cinder cone erupted a little more than 9,500 years ago.

Hike 25

PACIFIC CREST AND OBSIDIAN CLIFFS TRAILS

YAPOAH AND COLLIER CONES

View the High Cascades' youngest lavas and Oregon's longest (?) glacier, and return along the scenic Obsidian Cliffs.

DISTANCE ■ 14.8 miles

ELEVATION ■ 5,200 to 7,334 feet

DIFFICULTY ■ Moderate

TOPOGRAPHIC MAPS ■ Mt. Washington, North Sister, Black Crater, Trout Creek Butte

GEOLOGIC MAPS ■ 27, 30

PRECAUTIONS ■ A special permit is required to camp at Sunshine and to hike the flat Obsidian Trail; restricted use and limited access may apply to Obsidian Cliffs area. Weather can deteriorate quickly at high elevations. Requires shuttle vehicle at Frog Camp.

FOR INFORMATION ■ Sisters Ranger District, McKenzie Ranger District

About the Landscape: The youthful cinder cones at the northern end of the Three Sisters, including Yapoah, Four-in-One, and Collier Cones, are among the youngest vents in the Cascades. And on this hike, you can peer right into their navels.

Yapoah, a Native American term for an isolated hill, is a high-standing cinder cone between North Sister and McKenzie Pass. It erupted between 2,900 and 2,500 years ago, producing some of the lavas at McKenzie Pass. On Yapoah Cone, these lavas spill from their vent like jumbled bowels from a gash in the earth's fragile belly. This is a wonderful spot to examine lava *gutters,* pressure ridges, and the frozen relics of a volcanic throat. The rock is crumbly, sharp, and piled in unstable mounds.

Collier Cone may be the youngest lava vent in the Oregon Cascades. It erupted sometime between 500 and 2,500 years ago. Collier Cone produced lava flows that extend more than 8 miles east. Post-Pleistocene glacial advances of Collier Glacier have almost overridden the cone and deposited glacial erratic boulders on the cone's south shoulder. Collier Glacier, now in full retreat, still holds the official title as Oregon's longest glacier.

Trail Guide: Follow the Pacific Crest Trail from Lava Camp Lake south to the Cascades Lake Highway; complete the loop by returning on the Obsidian Cliffs Trail. An optional 1.6-mile side trip at Collier Cone and an optional overnight at Scott Spring can lengthen this hike. Leave shuttle vehicle at Frog Camp, eight miles west of Lava Lake Camp on Highway 242.

Begin at Lava Camp Lake Campground, approximately 1 mile east of McKenzie Pass on Highway 242 (McKenzie Pass Highway). The trailhead, to the west of the main campground, is marked for the Pacific Crest Trail (PCT).

Follow the marked spur trail about 0.5 mile westward to its junction with the PCT. The two trails meet at the edge of the lava flow from Yapoah Crater—a cinder cone that birthed much of the rugged basalt lava at McKenzie Pass. This lava flow towers above the trail. Take the PCT south. It veers from the lava flow and leads through moss-draped forest of fir and spruce, heading for Matthieu Lakes. At 1 mile, the inviting, straight, flat trail to Matthieu Lakes turns right and the PCT bends left. Take the PCT left and upward. It rises along the flanks of several cinder cones, and is well worth the investment of energy.

At 2.9 miles the PCT meets the North Matthieu Lake trail and South Matthieu Lake; stay on the PCT. Just south of the lake, the PCT intersects the Scott Pass Trail; again, stay on the PCT. From this junction, the PCT travels along the brink of a small unnamed cinder cone with flattened lava bombs that sometimes look like petrified cowpies, navigates the eastern margin of the Yapoah Crater flow, and rises along Yapoah Cone to cross at the vent for the Yapoah Crater flow.

At about 6 miles into the hike, the PCT winds along the north flank of Collier Cone, crossing Oppie Dilldock Pass amid the basalt lava flows. Informal trails invite you to explore the interior of Collier Cone. The most recommended path heads across the floor of the breached cone and climbs to the south cinder-cone rim, providing unparalleled views of Collier Glacier, the high lateral moraines of the glacier, the glacial moraine that veneers the side of Collier Cone—and the glacial erratics left on the top of the ridge here, and the glacial cirques that blister North Sister's north side. Return the way you came to the PCT to complete this 1.6-mile side trip.

From Collier Cone, the PCT skirts Little Brother and finds the popular Sunshine camping area below Scott Spring, at 9 miles from the Lava Camp Lake trailhead. The area around Scott Spring—an open, tree-lined flat known as Sunshine—is a good camping site, and an extremely popular one.

At Scott Spring, the Obsidian Cliffs Trail to Frog Camp turns west; take this route to return to the McKenzie Pass Highway. The trail parallels a glassy obsidian flow that forms Obsidian Cliffs, crosses the rough basalt flow of Collier Cone, and leads to Frog Camp in 5.8 miles from the junction with the PCT.

LAVA RIVER TRAIL

Lava Fields of McKenzie Pass

View young lava flows from Yapoah and South Belknap Craters on a handicapped-accessible trail.

DISTANCE ■ **0.5-mile loop**

ELEVATION ■ **5,324 to 5,350 feet**

DIFFICULTY ■ **Easy**

TOPOGRAPHIC MAP ■ **Mt. Washington**

GEOLOGIC MAPS ■ **27, 30**

PRECAUTIONS ■ **Other maps that may be useful include Three Sisters Wilderness/Mt. Washington Wilderness, Deschutes National Forest, and Willamette National Forest.**

FOR INFORMATION ■ **Sisters Ranger District**

About the Landscape: The black terrain of McKenzie Pass looks bleak. We are accustomed to landscapes smothered in plants. This barren, rocky pass, the lowest Cascade portal from eastern Oregon to the west, ushered pioneer wagons into the Willamette Valley in the 1890s. Disconnected relicts of the original road still remain, visible along the Lava River Trail. Geologically, the trail reveals long-frozen lava streams that flowed from Belknap Crater and South Belknap and Yapoah Cones, swirling as fiery rivers toward Sisters and the Deschutes plains. The age of these young-looking lava flows ranges from about 3,000 to 1,500 years.

Belknap Crater is a shield volcano. The Belknap Crater lava flows to the north and west are about 2,900 years in age. They lie atop cinders and flows erupted during the last 8,000 years. Lavas from Belknap Crater flowed more than 12 miles westward and probably also covered the McKenzie Pass area.

Trail Guide: The hike along the paved, 0.5-mile-long Lava River Trail loop is adjacent to the highway; the trail is handicapped-accessible.

This short hike begins and ends at McKenzie Pass on Highway 242. The trailhead is just east of the rock-walled Dee Wright Observatory. The Lava River Trail follows a basalt flow that originated at Yapoah Cone 2,600 years ago. The trail engages the lava field, including an elongated lava tube that has collapsed and several small pressure ridges. It climbs to a high point on a lava levee, where the lava spilled out of its main channel and pressure on the levee cracked it open. The trail winds through this cracked levee, revealing the columnar joints and cooling cracks within it.

From the top of the levee, the Lava River Trail provides a panoramic view of the dark lava fields of McKenzie Pass and the High Cascades.

North and Middle Sisters rise above the lava fields of McKenzie Pass.

115

MOUNT MAZAMA
AND THE MAKING OF CRATER LAKE

The deepest lake in Oregon once ranked among the Cascades' highest peaks. In the time of the glaciers and quick-flowing torrents, this was not Crater Lake but a multi-spired volcano known as Mount Mazama. Its summit reached at least 11,800 feet, higher than today's Mount Hood, and Mazama was more massive than Mount Jefferson. But Mount Mazama is no more. In its stead there is a hole filled with water—the third-deepest lake in the world, 1,932 feet from the waterline to its mysterious bottom.

Mount Mazama first erupted 400,000 years ago in the midst of the Pleistocene (the Ice Age). At least five sizable stratovolcanos once clustered together in one massive mountain. The oldest of these early volcanos is called Phantom Cone. Its remnants are exposed low on Dutton Cliff along the south shore of Crater Lake. The Phantom Ship, a ragged vessel of rock at the southeast shore of Crater Lake, is a remnant of the central vent system and feeder dikes for this oldest part of Mount Mazama.

The lavas of Mount Scott, just southeast of Crater Lake, may be the same age. Many other eruptions constructed a very complex mountain. By the end of the Pleistocene, 10,000 years ago, Mount Mazama formed a cluster of overlapping, eroded volcanic cones.

About 7,000 years ago, a few hundred years before Crater Lake was born, Mount Mazama erupted a viscous, silica-rich lava called *rhyodacite.* The great cliffs at Llao Rock are formed from a single flow that filled its own volcanic crater with at least a quarter cubic mile of hot, silica-rich paste. The last batch of this stuff made it to the surface just days before the climactic eruptions, and is called the Cleetwood Flow. The top of the Cleetwood Flow, on the north side of Crater Lake at Cleetwood Cove, was still soft when the rock fragments from Crater Lake's explosive eruptions hit it.

Were it not for these oozing rhyodacites, Mount Mazama might have been a better-behaved, more sedate volcano. But the escape of more than 3 cubic miles of pasty lava decreased the pressure in the magma chamber below. It was like taking the lid off a well-shaken pop bottle. Gases, mostly steam and carbon dioxide, effervesced and unleashed an explosive eruption.

The climactic eruption of Mount Mazama developed in four stages. It began dramatically with a towering, turbulent plume of coarse ash and hot gas. The first stages of the eruption probably resembled Mount St. Helens' 1980 eruption.

In the second phase, the ongoing eruption enlarged the vent. The

The Phantom Ship at Crater Lake

towering column began to collapse. Ash flows—thick, molten clouds moving at 100 mph with a temperature of 800 degrees Centigrade—blasted from the central vent. This phase of the eruption created the Wineglass welded tuff which today forms salmon-colored outcrops exposed along the trail to Grotto Cove and the boat dock.

In the third phase the roof of the chamber began to collapse along a circular system of cracks, from which Crater Lake has inherited its rounded

117

shape. Finally, more ash flows erupted from these cracks—at temperatures of 850 to 970 degrees Centigrade and speeds of 100 to 150 mph. As the eruption emptied the bowels of Mount Mazama, it sucked up the iron-rich basalts in the dregs of the magma chamber. The basalt from the bottom of the chamber now appears as the dark caps on the Pinnacles.

By the end of the eruption, almost 13 cubic miles of once-solid rock had vanished. And in its place was an awesome hole, a classic stratovolcano caldera nearly 4,000 feet deep. Wizard Island and Merriam Cone, a smaller volcano on the north floor of the *caldera,* have erupted since the climactic caldera collapse. Hot springs and geothermal prospects also indicate that the heat of an active volcano has not been completely shut off.

Today, Crater Lake harbors the most tantalizingly inaccessible geology in the Cascades. Precipitous cliffs archive its rocks. Crater Lake's national park status permits hiking off road and off trail, but also discourages such use with good reason: hazards to human life as well as to the spectacular geology and a fragile alpine ecosystem.

MOUNT SCOTT

THE SURVIVOR

Ascend the oldest (and only) remaining peak of the original Mount Mazama.

DISTANCE ■ 5.1 miles

ELEVATION ■ 7,696 to 8,926 feet

DIFFICULTY ■ Moderate

TOPOGRAPHIC MAPS ■ Crater Lake East, Crater Lake West, Crater Lake National Park and Vicinity

GEOLOGIC MAP ■ 31

PRECAUTIONS ■ Use caution around the cliffs at Mount Scott's summit. Carry water.

FOR INFORMATION ■ Crater Lake National Park

About the Landscape: Mount Scott is the highest and oldest part of Mount Mazama. It once stood as a separate, scoria-topped peak on the side of a much larger volcano. Isolation served it well. A major portion of the Mount Scott cone survived both glaciation and the cataclysmic eruption of the larger volcano. Today, Scott still sits apart, but the recluse is king of the mountain.

Like most stratovolcanos of the High Cascades, including Mounts

Jefferson and Hood, Mount Scott is mostly composed of andesite. The eroded sides and slopes reveal layers of tawny gray andesite and reddish cinders. These andesites are among the oldest remaining rocks of Mount Mazama (or Crater Lake), dated at about 420,000 years.

Trail Guide: As the trail climbs the southern, exposed side of Mount Scott, both wind and sun apply their energy. On a warm day, this trail may be hot; on a cool day it will be windy.

The trail up Mount Scott begins on the far east side of Crater Lake National Park's Rim Drive.

The trail dips across a low, glacially carved depression at Mount Scott's base. It twists around to the peak's south side and begins a steady, gracefully switchbacked climb toward the summit. On the lower and mid-slopes, glacial polish and scouring have smoothed many outcrops. As the trail nears the summit, scoria and a light cap of Crater Lake pumice, a relatively light dusting from the catastrophic eruption 6,600 years ago, blanket rock exposures.

At a little over 2.5 miles, the summit is a platform of glacially scoured andesites with abrupt drop-offs to the rocky slopes below. A lookout roosts on the summit, providing a great overview of the area. Return along the same route.

Hike

28

THE WATCHMAN

ANDESITES ABOVE WIZARD ISLAND

Gain a bird's-eye view of Merriam Cone and the convoluted lavas of Wizard Island.

DISTANCE ■ **1.4 miles**

ELEVATION ■ **7,400 to 8,056 feet**

DIFFICULTY ■ **Easy**

TOPOGRAPHIC MAPS ■ **Crater Lake East, Crater Lake West, Crater Lake National Park and Vicinity**

GEOLOGIC MAP ■ **31**

PRECAUTIONS ■ **None**

FOR INFORMATION ■ **Crater Lake National Park**

About the Landscape: The Watchman is a thick andesite flow on the west rim of Crater Lake. Its summit provides telling views of Llao Rock, Wizard Island, and, like all high points around Crater Lake's rim, views of the High Cascades, from Mount Jefferson and Mount Hood in the north to

Shasta and Lassen in the south. From the Watchman, views of Llao Rock, Cleetwood Flow, and the lava flows of Wizard Island are especially note-worthy.

Trail Guide: On Crater Lake's west rim, the trail leaves from a parking lot below The Watchman.

The broad trail—actually an old road—traipses up a gradual slope. Large andesite boulders litter the sides of the path. At 200 yards along this old road the trail turns upslope and winds up at the south side of The Watch-man, achieving the lookout station at the top in 1.2 miles without encoun-tering many outcrops.

From the top, the line of crags that represent the feeder dikes for the Watchman flow appears to extend from Wizard Island to The Watchman. But these two rock formations are unrelated, and several hundred thousand years different in age. Wizard Island and Merriam Cone loom beneath The Watchman. Wizard Cone looks as though it erupted yesterday, although its actual age is about 6,000 years. Return as you came.

THE PINNACLES

Hike 29

MAZAMA'S LAST GASP

View fumaroles formed by one of the last ash flows from the culminating eruption of Mount Mazama.

DISTANCE ■ 0.7 mile

ELEVATION ■ 5,450 to 5,460 feet

DIFFICULTY ■ Easy

TOPOGRAPHIC MAPS ■ Crater Lake East, Crater Lake West, Crater Lake National Park and Vicinity

GEOLOGIC MAP ■ 31

PRECAUTIONS ■ None

FOR INFORMATION ■ Crater Lake National Park

About the Landscape: The Pinnacles are not quite what they seem. You would think that these spires are solid, pointy columns, erosion-proofed by some dark, resistant caprock. In fact, they are hollow, made erosion-proof from the inside out. The Pinnacles represent *fumaroles*—pipes or conduits through which hot gases trapped in this ash flow rose to the sur-face. Hollow tubes core each pinnacle. The hot gasses cemented the loose pumice around the flumes through which they rose, forming a very hard, resistant rock around a hollow conduit. This resistant rock remains

The Pinnacles are the hollow remains of fumaroles, conduits through which gases rose to the surface during Mount Mazama's last eruption.

today as a pinnacle, while the loose pumice and ash around it has been eroded by rain and the action of Sand Creek.

The ash flow in which The Pinnacles developed represents part of the culminating eruption of Mount Mazama. Each pinnacle displays a gradual transition from light-colored base to dark-colored top. This change in color is related to a change in the composition of the erupted pumice. As the frothing magma chamber of Mount Mazama emptied, the ash at the top of the chamber was light-colored and silica-rich; the bottom contained darker minerals and dark basalt magma. The result is the light bottoms—where the first ash fell—and dark tops—the basaltic dregs of the magma chamber bottom—of The Pinnacles.

Trail Guide: On the east side of Crater Lake National Park's Rim Drive, about 4 miles south of the Mount Scott trailhead, take the Lost Creek Campground road 5.7 miles to The Pinnacles viewpoint.

This is a great hike for those interested in Mount Mazama's last day. The short walkway along Sand Creek Canyon provides opportunities to peer over the rim, or sit and contemplate the view.

Chapter 6.

THE DESCHUTES BASIN

Cross-bedding, Deschutes Basin sediments, Cove Palisades

The Deschutes Basin provides a record of explosive eruptions from vanished volcanos: the flat, explosive volcanos of the Cascades that erupted from about 6 to 2 million years ago, and which are now covered by the High Cascade peaks.

Several older rhyolite domes and vents, including Smith Rock and Powell Butte, while geographically in the Deschutes Basin, have different geologic genetics. Technically, these Miocene and Oligocene rocks seem

JOINTS

They seem to be the most insignificant of things. Cracks in the rock. Geologists call them *joints.* Like wrinkles in a face, though, joints are an outcrop's biographer. They tell the story of heat and cooling, tension and stress, breaking and healing in the stone, and the stuff of which it is made. Without them, we would not recognize most rocks.

Basalts are defined by their columnar joints, which grow as a

Platy jointing in andesite

closely related to the Western Cascades. Their eruptions of ash contributed to the John Day Fossil Beds and Painted Hills, and their Oligocene contemporaries constructed the Western Cascades. But who would ever look for them in that category? So they have been adopted by adjoining regions, much like a neighbor might adopt the cat of a family that moved away. Some geologists toss them into the High Lava Plains. Others, including this one, consider them part of the Deschutes Basin.

molten lava flow cools. Basalt solidifies from the bottom upward. As the flow cools upward from the bottom, the joints, and thus the columns, propagate upward. And as the flow cools from the top down, joints radiate downward to find the coolest path.

In andesites columns display horizontal cracks that divide them into plates. This phenomenon is called *platy jointing.*

Granites and other plutonic igneous rocks also crack as they cool, producing geometric sets of joints. Individual cracks can extend for hundreds of yards. Joints also develop and expand as erosion strips the cover from a granite or other large body of plutonic rock.

Joints develop as the earth shifts, just as cracks develop in a foundation as the earth settles. The pattern of joints reveals the direction and magnitude of the stress that produced them. When stress becomes strong enough to move rocks then these simple cracks evolve into something more dynamic—a fault.

Columnar joints in basalt

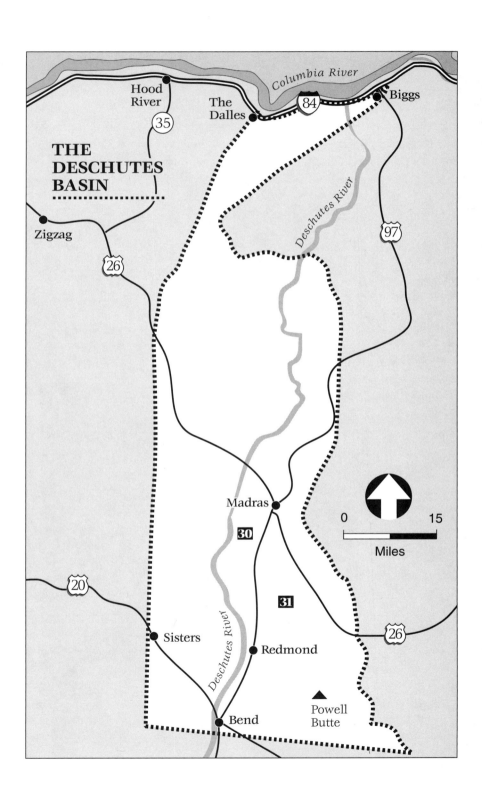

THE
DESCHUTES
BASIN

Columbia River

Hood
River

The
Dalles

Biggs

35

Deschutes River

97

Zigzag

26

Madras

30

31

20

Sisters

Redmond

Deschutes River

Powell
Butte

Bend

26

0   15
Miles

GEOLOGIC TIMETABLE 6: THE DESCHUTES BASIN		
Four significant events that shaped the landscape		
Millions of years ago	Geologic era	Geologic event
1.2	Pleistocene	Flows from Newberry Volcano choke Deschutes and Crooked Rivers
2–5	Pliocene	Ash-rich eruptions of early High Cascades deposit ash gravel, welded tuffs, and thin basalt flows
17	Miocene	Smith Rock tuff cone erupts
23	Oligocene	Powell Butte and other rhyolite domes formed

Hike 30

COVE PALISADES

THE COLORFUL CANYON

Visit a spectacular canyon cut into colored and columned cliffs, with a lake in the bottom.

DISTANCE ■ 2 miles

ELEVATION ■ 2,400 to 2,500

DIFFICULTY ■ Easy

TOPOGRAPHIC MAPS ■ Round Butte Dam, Culver

GEOLOGIC MAP ■ 32–34

PRECAUTIONS ■ This is a day-use fee area. As in all park areas, collecting rocks requires a permit and is for scholarly study only.

FOR INFORMATION ■ Cove Palisades State Park

About the Landscape: Tucked into the backcountry between Madras and Mount Jefferson is a raw wound cut by the Deschutes and Crooked Rivers into the fragile, stacked bedrock of the Deschutes Basin. The canyon's layered walls are composed of alternating ash beds, gravels, and lava flows.

The most spectacular features of this 300-foot-deep canyon are the intra-canyon flows of basalt from Newberry Volcano, about 1.2 million years in age. These basalts form the high columned cliffs that veneer the canyon's sides and also form The Island, a high, isolated finger of basalt that juts south from the center of Cove Palisades. The top of The Island interests ecologists because it is among the few places in central Oregon never grazed by domestic livestock, except briefly in the 1920s by a band of sheep whose owner kept them—and a whiskey still—active for several years atop The Island.

Near the campground, a spectacular, layered rock formation known as The Ship displays pastel layers that are ash-rich gravels, river sands, and welded ash-flow tuffs (*ignimbrites*). The sands and gravels were deposited

127

The Ship at Cove Palisades is an eroded stack of ash-flow tuffs and fine-grained sediments.

by braided streams from the Cascades. The pinkish layer is an ash-flow tuff that erupted as a hot cloud of molten ash and gas that probably moved at speeds in excess of 100 mph.

Trail Guide: To reach Cove Palisades, from Redmond take US 97 north 5 miles. Near the bottom of the north-facing downgrade from Juniper Butte, take the road to the left marked CULVER AND COVE PALISADES. In downtown Culver, turn left on Main Street and follow signs for Cove Palisades State

Park, 3 miles west. Drive through the park to the headquarters and camping area at the base of The Ship. The trailhead for day hikes is at the main park campground just below The Ship. At the registration kiosk, cross the road and turn right to head downhill.

Along the trail and to the left at the trail's beginning, coarse columnar jointed basalts of the Newberry basalt flow can be examined. The trail begins to drop toward Lake Billy Chinook, with a view of the columnar cliffs of The Island several hundred yards to the right. Note the 30- to 50-foot-long dome-shaped arches of the columns in the upper part of the island. These are good examples of inflated basalt—basalt that was supported by gas pressure as it cooled.

The trail system on this side of the road is a network of wide, easy paths. Most provide views of the surrounding canyon walls. Note especially that the column-rich Newberry flows are simply stuck on the sides of the canyon walls.

An informal trail leads to the top of The Island. It is steep, rugged, undeveloped, and hazardous. Inquire at the Cove Palisades State Park Headquarters about the trail condition and access before exploring this area. Return the way you came.

SMITH ROCK

THE TUFF CLIMBER'S DREAM

Walk among tuffs, Newberry basalts, and 18-million-year-old rhyolite in a climbers' paradise on the Crooked River.

DISTANCE ■ 5.5-mile loop

ELEVATION ■ 370 to 2,800 feet

DIFFICULTY ■ Moderate

TOPOGRAPHIC MAPS ■ Redmond, Opal City, Gray Butte, O'Neil

GEOLOGIC MAP ■ 35

PRECAUTIONS ■ This is a day-use fee area. Stay on the route described; other routes may result in being cliffed out, or requiring technical skills and equipment to descend rock ledges. Collecting rocks requires a permit.

FOR INFORMATION ■ Smith Rock State Park

About the Landscape: Smith Rock is a climbers' mecca. These gritty tuffs invite handholds and hammered supports. The scope of the rocks and of the Crooked River's winding course through the area provide a perspective that is both humbling and full of grandeur.

A climber finds a handhold on Smith Rock.

Smith Rock is only part of a much larger volcanic and sedimentary complex centered around Gray Butte to the northeast. The tan and buff Smith Rock tuff erupted about 17 million years ago. This small volcano coughed up a hot, pasty mixture of ash and steam that formed and flowed in thin layers before it cooled and solidified. The vent area may have been near today's popular Smith Rock climbing area. The gas-charged eruptions carried chunks of the underlying bedrock up the volcanic conduit. The holes in the rock walls today are cavities left when these chunks of rock erode, and/or when gas pockets where frothy tuff collected are hollowed out by water and wind. In many parts of Smith Rock State Park the crude layering created by multiple eruptions of sticky tuff is evident.

The Crooked River flows past the rhyolite dike that intrudes Smith Rock tuff.

The darker red rock that forms a picturesque maroon spire and magenta laces across the vertical walls is rhyolite. It intruded through the tuff cone. Close examination reveals vertical banding in this rhyolite—a relic of its upward flow.

A dark-rimmed basalt plateau frames the riverbank on the south side of Smith Rock. These basalts flowed from Newberry Crater, filling the ancestral Crooked River Canyon about 1.2 million years ago. The Crooked River recarved its channel through these thick basalts during the Pleistocene (Ice Age).

Trail Guide: The hike around Smith Rock explores the Smith Rock tuff. The overlook where the trail plunges down to Crooked River provides a vista of the tawny Smith Rock tuffs just across the river, of the red spire of rhyolite dike—the dark pinnacle at the first river bend, of the Newberry basalts that the overlook is built on, and of the oldest rocks here—the 18-million-year-old rhyolite of Gray Butte just below the basalt at this overlook.

To reach Smith Rock State Park, from US 97 in Terrebonne, turn east onto B Street. Cross the railroad tracks, go down a hill and then turn left on First Street. In 0.5 mile turn right onto Wilcox, drive 1 mile and turn left onto Smith Rock Loop. Reach the park in about 2 miles. From the parking lot, asphalt paths lead to the trailhead.

The trail leads downslope and across the Crooked River. Just across the bridge, follow the trail upstream along the Crooked River. The buff and magenta cliffs that rise to your left are Smith Rock tuff laced with veins of red rhyolite. At 0.75 mile the main trail continues upslope past basalt rimrock to the right. On this slope the trail is a scramble that leads to a roadway (locally called the Burma Road) which briefly follows an irrigation canal (the North Unit canal) and provides a switchbacked path to the Smith Rock ridge crest, about 2 miles from the bridge crossing.

The ridge crest rewards the hiker with a climber's-eye view. Along this ridge you can glimpse streaks of iron oxide that tint the rocks red, and examine the inclusions that create knobs and holes. To the north, 1 mile across Sherwood Canyon, multiple horns of Smith Rock tuff emerge from the ridge.

From this point, an informal climbers' trail plunges down the rocky but hikeable back side of Smith Rock. In 0.5 mile look carefully for a spur trail to the north. This unmarked trail provides a rough but hikeable 1-mile route back to the Crooked River and the main trail along the base of Smith Rock. The river trail leads from the west side of Smith Rock back to the bridge and trailhead.

Chapter 7.
THE HIGH LAVA PLAINS

Spatter cone, Diamond Craters

In Oregon, the High Lava Plains is the land of the laconic geologist. Out here, just two words will get you by: rhyolite and basalt. The High Lava Plains is, very simply, a wide belt of small rhyolite and basalt volcanos that stretch from south of Burns to south of Bend. Most Oregonians call the area the High Desert. It follows the Brothers fault zone at the northern edge of the Basin and Range.

The most curious thing about the High Lava Plains volcanos is their ages. Generally, the oldest ones (Beatty's Butte, 10.4 million years) are on the east end. The ages of the volcanos and eruptions grow progressively

LOOKING AT LAVAS:
THE BIOGRAPHY OF A VOLCANIC ROCK

While volcanic rocks may seem complicated, each wears its heart on its sleeve. Their textures and colors tell their eruptive history. Some biographical details you can use to unravel a rock's story include:

Vesicles. The tiny holes in most volcanic rocks are the heritage of gas bubbles—like the bubbles in a soda pop or beer. As the lava solidifies, gas is trapped as bubbles and creates small holes in the rocks we see today. Vesicles are often more abundant at the top of a lava flow. They may be elongate or ellipsoidal parallel to the direction of flow. And in rare cases, where the flow was stagnant as the gas escaped, they are elongate upward.

Pillows. When hot basalt lava flows into water, it chills rapidly into rounded shapes called pillows or *pillow lava.* Pillows usually have a glassy rim and radial cracks. Pillow basalts may be far from water today, but when they were molten, they flowed into the sea or into a lake where they chilled and solidified.

Phenocrysts. Volcanic rocks are very fine-grained because they chill quickly, with no time for crystals to grow. But sometimes, even in the seemingly finest-grained rocks, a larger crystal will glint on a fresh surface. These bigger crystals are called *phenocrysts* (Greek for "visible crystal"). The large crystals grew slowly in the magma chamber beneath the volcano. They were carried up and erupted with the lava. And once spewed from its warm, magmatic womb, the lava cooled and crystallized quickly, creating a fine-grained matrix for the large crystals that it carried.

younger to the west. The youngest vent system is Newberry Volcano, just south of Bend, which birthed the Big Obsidian Flow only 1,300 years ago. Geologists are unsure of the reason for this neat progression of volcanism across Oregon's midriff. The best explanation seems to be that the Brothers fault zone has opened access to the earth's mantle, rather like a zipper opening steadily from Burns to Bend. Alternative ideas include the steepening of the subduction zone off the Oregon coast, and the clockwise rotation of the Cascade Range.

The most visible rocks of the High Lava Plains are basalt flows and

Vesicles in basalt

rhyolite domes. The domes include Glass Buttes (6 million years old), Quartz Mountain and Pine Mountain (about 1 million years old), and China Hat (800,000 years old). Gas-laden rhyolite tuff eruptions produced Fort Rock and Hole in the Ground less than 1 million years ago.

NEWBERRY VOLCANO

Although Newberry Volcano is within geologic spitting distance of the High Cascades, Newberry is not a Cascade volcano. It is not produced by the subduction zone, as are the Cascades. Instead, Newberry Volcano is the youngest recognized eruptive center of Oregon's High Lava Plains. This classic, low-slung shield volcano covers 500 square miles. Most of Newberry's flows are basalt, but there are other features as well. The volcano has peppered its flanks with more than 400 cinder cones. And glassy, wrinkled obsidian flows tumble from the crater rim into the volcano's crater.

Newberry first erupted 1.2 million years ago, producing lava and ash. The collapse of its caldera to form Paulina Lake and East Lake occurred at least 200,000 years ago. The best known features of Newberry Volcano have erupted during the last 12,000 years. These include The Dome (11,200 years ago), Lava Cast Forest (6,150 years ago), Lava Butte (6,190 years ago), and Big Obsidian Flow (1,300 years ago).

Newberry Volcano. The Big Obsidian Flow is visible at upper right. (Photo courtesy of Oregon Dept. of Transportation)

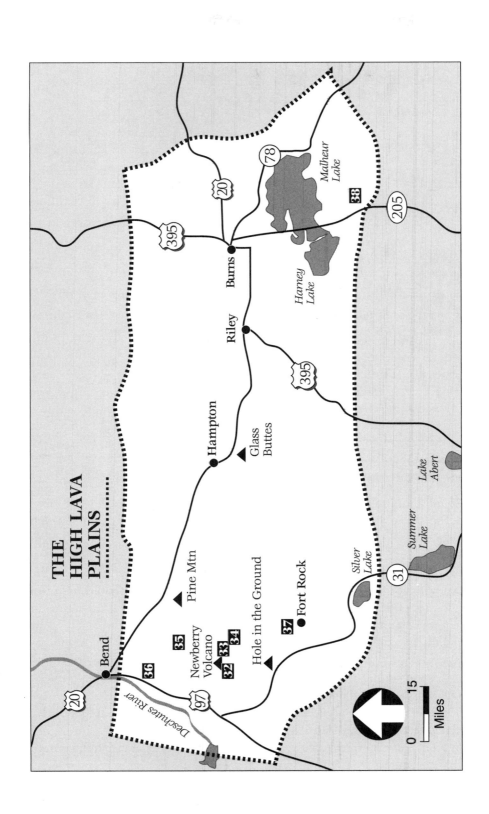

GEOLOGIC TIMETABLE 7: THE HIGH LAVA PLAINS

Five significant events that shaped the landscape

Millions of years ago	Geologic era	Geologic event
0.0013 (1,300 years ago)	Holocene	Big Obsidian Flow, Newberry Volcano
0.010 (10,000 years ago)	Pleistocene	Fort Rock tuff cone erupts in Pleistocene lake
0.017 (17,000 years ago)	Pleistocene	Diamond Craters erupt
1.2	Pleistocene	First eruptions of Newberry Volcano
10.6	Miocene	Earliest High Lava Plains volcanism at Beattys Butte

Hike
32

PAULINA PEAK TRAIL

OVERVIEW OF A CALDERA

Ascend to the rim of Newberry Volcano for views of the High Cascades, Paulina and East Lakes, and the Big Obsidian Flow.

DISTANCE ■ 5 miles

ELEVATION ■ 6,400 to 7,484 feet

DIFFICULTY ■ Strenuous

TOPOGRAPHIC MAPS ■ Paulina Peak, East Lake

GEOLOGIC MAPS ■ 36, 37

PRECAUTIONS ■ This trail follows rimrocks; cliffs drop steeply in some places.

FOR INFORMATION ■ Newberry National Volcanic Monument

About the Landscape: Newberry Volcano's crater was created by a collapse of the shield volcano's summit area about 200,000 years ago. Since then, the volcano has sporadically tried to fill in the hole with rhyolite, obsidian, and tuff. The eruptions built up the land area in the central part of Newberry Crater, dividing what had been one lake into two. The area between Paulina and East Lakes is the product of eruptions that lasted from 7,300 to 7,100 years ago. These eruptions produced the central cone and several rhyolite domes and obsidian flows. Two obsidian flows (Game Hut and Crater obsidian flows) emanate from this cone and are the same age (about 7,300 years). The Interlake obsidian flow occupies the north end of this area and extends to both Paulina and East Lakes. It is the youngest part of this central area, erupting 7,100 years ago.

Paulina Peak also affords a view of the Big Obsidian Flow just to the east. This flow is dated at 1,300 years—Oregon's youngest known lava flow. Semicircular pressure ridges and elongate flow gutters indicate the direction of the flow and its complex patterns.

138

Trail Guide: To reach the trailhead, just inside the official entry station for Newberry National Volcanic Monument at Paulina Lake, turn right on Paulina Peak Road. About 0.7 mile along this road, turn left into a small gravel parking area labeled PAULINA PEAK TRAILHEAD.

The trail rises sharply for 100 yards, then eases along a ridge crest. Red tuff, product of very old (300,000 years?) Newberry eruptions, appears in low outcrops along the trail's edge. At about 1 mile into the hike, the trail crosses into a gray rhyolite unit. This rock forms the cliffs of Paulina Peak and supports its steep slopes. For the next mile, the trail rises steeply, veering occasionally to the edge of cliffs for a view of East Lake and the imposing sides of Paulina Peak. The trail flattens near the crest of the peak and crosses thick accumulations of pumice deposited by the eruption of the Big Obsidian Flow. At 2 miles into the hike, the trail intersects the Paulina Road trail (trail 58). Keep straight ahead on the North Paulina Peak Trail, another 0.5 mile to the summit.

When you have had your fill of scenery, return as you came. (For a longer walk on a gentler grade, hike along Paulina Peak Road 4 miles to the trailhead.)

Hike
33

BIG OBSIDIAN FLOW

OREGON'S YOUNGEST KNOWN LAVA FLOW

A short, well-developed path reveals the texture, colors, and origin of this glassy volcanic flow.

DISTANCE ■ **1 mile**

ELEVATION ■ **6,400 to 6,500 feet**

DIFFICULTY ■ **Easy**

TOPOGRAPHIC MAPS ■ **Paulina Peak, East Lake**

GEOLOGIC MAPS ■ **36, 37**

PRECAUTIONS ■ **Newberry National Volcanic Monument has an entrance fee. Volcanic glass is very sharp! At the beginning of the climb, there is a 50-foot-high metal staircase.**

FOR INFORMATION ■ **Newberry National Volcanic Monument**

About the Landscape: This trail takes you on an Alice in Wonderland–like trip through the fifth-largest obsidian flow in North America. The gray, black, and red rocks on this flow are glassy and extremely variable. The glassy nature of obsidian is created by the very rapid solidification of a super-heated, pasty rhyolite. When rhyolite erupts, the surface of the flow solidifies so quickly that no crystals have time to form. Instead, the rock chills as glass.

Trail Guide: To reach the trailhead, drive to the official entry station for Newberry National Volcanic Monument at Paulina Lake. Continue on County Road 21 around the south shore of Paulina Lake. The marked turn-off is the on the right about 1 mile east of the entry station.

The trail leads about 50 feet up a staircase to the top of the flow's steep front. Once you have scaled the stairs, the rest of the hike is easy, relatively level, and on a well-developed trail complete with benches and interpretive

Flow banding in the Big Obsidian Flow

signs. There is lots to see on this short hike: The color of the obsidian varies from black to light gray as more water—in the form of microscopic bubbles—was incorporated in the rock. Where steam surged through the glassy flow, oxidizing the microscopic iron particles in the cooling obsidian, the rock is a red-brown color. In places along the trail, swirls that look like patterns in taffy show the direction the lava was flowing when it chilled abruptly into solid glass. When you reach trail's end, return along the loop to the trailhead.

Hike

34

THE DOME

A BREACHED CINDER CONE

The Dome is not a solid rhyolite geologic dome but a well-rounded cinder cone.

DISTANCE ■ **3 miles**

ELEVATION ■ **6,950 to 7,150 feet**

DIFFICULTY ■ **Easy**

TOPOGRAPHIC MAP ■ **East Lake**

GEOLOGIC MAPS ■ **36, 37**

PRECAUTIONS ■ **None**

FOR INFORMATION ■ **Newberry National Volcanic Monument**

About the Landscape: The Dome is a young cinder cone near the summit of a 300,000-year-old volcano. It represents Newberry Volcano's first eruptive episode after the Ice Age, dated at 11,200 years. Like a young child afraid of heights or open places, The Dome teeters on the brink of the desert, clinging to the sparsely forested side of its Mother Newberry.

The Dome opens to the east, allowing basalt lavas to flow from the open side. This opening, or horseshoe shape, is called a *breach*. The Dome, technically, is a breached cinder cone. A hike around The Dome's rim reveals the cinder cone's interior--layers of red-brown lava, *volcanic bombs,* and unconsolidated cinders. The dark surface of The Dome is veneered with gray pumice from Big Obsidian Flow's eruptions—providing a deceptively light color to this basaltic cinder cone.

Trail Guide: To reach the trailhead, from the official entry station for Newberry National Volcanic Monument at Paulina Lake, drive about 5 miles to the end of the Newberry Crater road (County Road 21), turn east, uphill, on USFS Road 21 (China Cap Road), and drive 2.5 miles. The trailhead is on the right at a subtly marked turnout.

The 0.75-mile trail to the top of The Dome rises in short switchbacks through sparse vegetation. The barren, crescent-shaped summit of The Dome invites a 0.75-mile walk around the rim. A few examples of aerodynamic geology—volcanic bombs—lie on the rim's surface. Other bombs tempt from below. But remember that an easy hike down in these unconsolidated cinders requires a difficult struggle to regain the summit. After your circuit of the rim, return the way you came.

LAVA CAST FOREST TRAIL

Hike 35

TREE MOLDS IN PAHOEHOE

This fossil forest is a rather Zen concept—a forest represented by the vacant hollows where there used to be trees.

DISTANCE ■ 2-mile loop

ELEVATION ■ 4,750 to 4,800 feet

DIFFICULTY ■ Easy

TOPOGRAPHIC MAP ■ Lava Cast Forest

GEOLOGIC MAPS ■ 36, 37

PRECAUTIONS ■ Entry road is washboarded by midsummer; allow plenty of time (30 minutes) for the drive on USFS roads.

FOR INFORMATION ■ La Pine Recreation Area

About the Landscape: Lava Cast Forest is a misnomer—these are hollow *molds* of tree trunks. Lava molds form when lavas are cool enough to flow around and chill (solidify) against a tree, but still so hot that they set the tree on fire. Considering that this basalt solidified at about 1,000 degrees Centigrade (about 1,900 degrees Fahrenheit), it is no wonder that nearly solid lava could ignite anything that it touched. This forest burned as the lava flowed through it.

This missing forest is the product of a basalt flow from Newberry Volcano's Northwest Rift zone. The age of this flow is about 6,000 years, based on carbon-14 dates of charcoal from the burned trees. The direction that the lava moved is preserved in many vertical molds. The lava piled up on the upstream side of the trees, leaving a mold that is slightly higher and thicker on the uphill side of the tree toward the lava's vent. The horizontal tree molds here most likely developed as the trees fell from their burned stumps into the flowing lava below.

Trail Guide: From milepost 153 on US 97 at the turnoff to Sunriver (west), turn east on USFS Road 9720, marked LAVA CAST FOREST. Follow this gravel road 8.5 miles to USFS 9720-950—Lava Cast Forest Road—and drive another 0.5 mile to the parking area and trailhead.

This handicapped-accessible walk is a 2-mile loop on a paved trail. It is interesting to compare the diameter of the pines that were standing at the time of the lava flow with the size of the present old-growth trees, and to close your eyes and visualize what the old forest must have looked like before and during the eruption.

Tree molds in the Lava Cast Forest

TRAIL OF THE MOLTEN LAND

Hike 36

LAVA LANDS VISITOR CENTER

A very civilized hiking experience offers a fine introduction to the mechanics of lava flows.

DISTANCE ■ 1-mile loop
ELEVATION ■ 4,500 to 4,650 feet
DIFFICULTY ■ Easy
TOPOGRAPHIC MAP ■ Lava Butte
GEOLOGIC MAPS ■ 36, 37
PRECAUTIONS ■ None
FOR INFORMATION ■ Fort Rock Ranger District

About the Landscape: Lava Butte is part of Newberry Volcano's Northwest Rift zone. Although very close to the High Cascades, this cinder cone is a child of the High Lava Plains, not the Cascades.

About 7,000 years ago, fissure eruptions (lava fountains) developed along the line of faults known as Newberry's Northwest Rift zone. By about 6,500 years ago, the Lava Butte cinder cone was built. Then another pulse of fluid basalt magma about 6,200 years ago burst through the side of the cinder cone, creating the Lava Butte flow. This basalt flow extends to the Deschutes River. It dammed the ancestral river, creating a lake that backed up the Deschutes past Sun River almost to La Pine. As the lake drained, the Deschutes cut a new channel which it now follows.

Trail Guide: The trail begins from the Lava Lands Visitor Center—headquarters for Newberry National Volcanic Monument—on US 97 11 miles south of Bend. The visitor center provides background information about the geology, ecology, and human history of the area. During the summer, competent volunteers provide hourly tours and geologic interpretation. The bus ride up Lava Butte offers a good overview of the lava flow.

From the visitor center, the handicapped-accessible loop trail winds through the 6,200-year-old lava flow that erupted from the base of Lava Butte. It showcases features of the flow (lava balls, pressure ridges, columnar joints, gutters, levees, and others) through a series of well-placed interpretive signs.

FORT ROCK

While Newberry Volcano looks suspiciously like the Cascades, Fort Rock is unmistakably part of the High Lava Plains. This is clearly desert. Many features, including Hole in the Ground and Fort Rock, are surrounded by sagebrush and irrigated alfalfa fields. Fort Rock provides an example of the rhyolite-rich lavas of the High Lava Plains. This ring of volcanic tuff rises 300 feet, a monument to fire and water. Its eruption was only the first part of Fort Rock's creation. Today the most important force in the continuing genesis and sculpting of this desert landform is water.

Its circular structure was hewn into today's familiar semicircle by the unrelenting action of a huge lake. In the Pleistocene, Oregon's desert floor was awash in six huge lakes from Fort Rock east to the Owyhees. The lake that surrounded Fort Rock covered 585 square miles and was about 100 feet deep. The tuff ring rose as an island in 50 feet of water. The prevailing southeast winds drove against the soft tuff, wearing away the wall and creating the semicircular opening.

Today, wave-cut terraces surround Fort Rock, and even appear in its interior. The terraces are especially notable on the south and east sides near Fort Rock State Park. The lake waters were at their highest level about 20,000 years ago, and water lapped at Fort Rock's feet until about 13,000 years ago. Fort Rock Cave, in a nearby tuff ring, has yielded human artifacts (sandals) dated at 13,200 years in age.

Fort Rock is a tuff cone that erupted into a Pleistocene lake.

THE WAVE-CUT CONE

AN ANCIENT LAKE'S SCULPTURE

Explore a desert volcano whose most important ingredient was water.

DISTANCE ■ 1 mile

ELEVATION ■ 4,350 to 4,500 feet

DIFFICULTY ■ Easy

TOPOGRAPHIC MAP ■ Fort Rock

GEOLOGIC MAP ■ 1

PRECAUTIONS ■ None

FOR INFORMATION ■ Fort Rock State Park

About the Landscape: Fort Rock is a tuff ring and, based on its form and degree of erosion, is probably between 50,000 and 100,000 years old (Pleistocene). Like other tuff rings on Oregon's High Lava Plains, Fort Rock was built by explosive, gas-charged eruptions of frothy lava and water-laden ash. Instead of producing a solid flow (like Big Obsidian Flow), the frothy lava erupted hot, gooey ash. This ash plopped out of a ring-shaped circular vent, creating a ring of porous tuff. The fine bedding in Fort Rock's walls represents layers of sticky tuff.

Trail Guide: To reach Fort Rock, from US 97 near La Pine, take Highway 31 approximately 20 miles east and turn north onto County Road 5-12C (Cabin Lake Road). Drive 3 miles to downtown Fort Rock. Follow signs 1.5 miles to Fort Rock State Park.

From the parking area, informal trails lead through Fort Rock. The most obvious path provides a quick scramble up to the flat wave-cut bench just above the kiosk. The notch here was carved by the waves of the huge Pleistocene lake that once surrounded this horse-shoe shaped relic.

From the wave-cut bench a mile-long loop follows the interior of Fort Rock. At the beginning of this walk large, oddly shaped holes are evident on the north wall; these are mostly enlarged, eroded gas pockets, although a few once housed angular stones that the explosive magma ripped from underlying bedrock. About 0.25 mile farther along the northwest wall, the steep interior cliffs showcase the layers left by the repeated belches of gloppy gas-laden ash and lava (about the same consistency as fresh cowpies) that built Fort Rock. The layers indicate that a rapid succession of coughs and belches, not just one traumatic upheaval, created Fort Rock. Note that the layers slope down toward the center, or vent area, of Fort Rock. In some areas, especially on the north and west interior walls, the layers display droops, bends, folds, cross-bedding, and other "sedimentary"

Wave-cut bench above the parking area at Fort Rock State Park

structures which indicate each was deposited as a very thick, plastic mass that deformed under its own weight and the dictates of gravity.

About 0.5 mile from the parking area, the path reaches the west side of Fort Rock. Here several earlier wave-cut benches are evident, as well as more strongly layered tuff. Water once reached high in the interior of Fort Rock, creating huge piles of rubble. From the west side, a road heads downhill, and branches to the south, reaching the southeast bench in about 0.25 mile. After touring the well-developed terraces on the southeast side, where at least three different lake levels can be deciphered, follow the roadway 0.25 mile back to the trailhead and picnic area.

DIAMOND CRATERS

Diamond Craters, which erupted 17,000 and 15,000 years ago, rank among the youngest basalts in southeastern Oregon. The first eruptions spread a layer of hard, impermeable basalt like a thick blanket over the area. During the second phase of Diamond Craters activity, basalt lava was injected beneath this blanket, but could not erupt. Consequently, the area began to dome upward like a doughnut overstuffed with custard.

You can only overfill a doughnut for so long before something happens. In the case of Diamond Craters, several things happened. Eruptions of *pahoehoe* lava squirted out on the south side, creating Lava Pit Crater and the surrounding flows and craters. The bulging top of the dome collapsed, creating a valley (or *graben*) across the center of the Diamond Craters area; and other eruptions, including explosions that produced only gas and left only a crater (*maar*), pockmarked the large dome area.

Joints in the basalt at Diamond Craters

LAVA PIT, RED BOMB, AND TWIN CRATERS

DIAMOND CRATERS NATURAL AREA

Take a look at pahoehoe *and* aa *lava flows, a cinder cone, several craters,* graben, *and* maars.

Hike 38

DISTANCE ■ 4 miles

ELEVATION ■ 4,900 to 5,200 feet

DIFFICULTY ■ Easy

TOPOGRAPHIC MAPS ■ Diamond Swamp, Diamond

GEOLOGIC MAP ■ 1

PRECAUTIONS ■ Do not collect or damage plants, animals, or rocks in this BLM natural area. Bring plenty of water. This is a desert area with no trees—and no toilet facilities, either. Some cross-country hiking is necessary to see all features; a detailed brochure is available at the Hines BLM office 5 miles west of Burns or at a kiosk at Lava Pit Crater.

FOR INFORMATION ■ Hines Bureau of Land Management office

About the Landscape: Along much of Highway 205 east of US 20, the red-brown, coarsely columned cliffs are Devine Canyon ash flow, a 9-million-year-old volcanic formation that erupted from vents near Burns. At Lava Pit Crater, note the flow patterns frozen into the lavas, including exquisite lava gutters, tubes, and ropy pahoehoe festooned and wrinkled as the flowing lava formed a glass skin and solidified.

Trail Guide: The hike mostly follows a gravel road with side excursions to visit specific features. To reach Diamond Craters Natural Area, from Burns take US 20 east 2 miles to Highway 205, then drive south 40.5 miles to the Diamond Grain Camp Road. Drive east 6 miles, then turn north and drive 2 miles to Diamond Craters Natural Area. The hike around Diamond Craters begins at the Lava Pit Crater parking lot 0.6 mile into the Diamond Craters Natural Area.

Begin your hike with a tour of the multiple lava pits at the first stop. The surface of this *pahoehoe* lava is fragile, so please be careful. Also, the rims of these craters are undercut and unsupported; stifle the urge to run to the edge and peer over, or you could become the latest addition to the rubble on the crater floor. Continue another 0.6 mile along the road to Red Bomb Crater. This cone is constructed of red cinders or scoria. Many volcanic bombs are scattered here. Remember this is a geologic catch-and-release area: don't take any souvenirs home with you.

Continue 2.7 miles along the roadway to Twin Craters. These symmetrical craters are *maars*—blowouts created by an eruption or explosion of

A pahoehoe *swirl at Diamond Craters*

steam. The road ends at Dry Maar at the edge of the Central Crater Complex about 0.6 mile farther. This complex was a main part of the collapse as lava escaped from under the inflated dome at the eruption site—Lava Pit Crater. This crater complex is really a collapsed caldera, similar to Crater Lake but smaller (200 feet deep and 3,500 feet wide) and softer in outline, with many smaller nested craters.

To return, you may retrace your steps, or you may scale the central ridge and return cross-country along the north side of the Central Crater Complex and then 0.25 mile west along the margin of a narrow valley, the graben created by collapse of the basalt crust of Diamond Craters.

Chapter 8.
THE BASIN AND RANGE

Mudcracks in the arid Basin and Range

Oregon's Basin and Range specializes in open space, an arid climate, and huge fault-block mountains: Steens Mountain, Abert Rim, Hart Mountain, and the Pueblos. Thermal springs and earthquakes energize this region, which extends from Klamath Falls almost to the Idaho border, hanging like a skirt below the High Lava Plains volcanics.

This is the home of the young and the restless, where the mantle rises closest to the surface and the continent moves and stretches. The uneven tableau of basins and flat-topped ranges are the stretch marks of a continent birthing new land. Until about 16 million years ago, this was a flat, arid, basalt-drowned landscape. Then, gradually, the faults of the northern Basin and Range in Oregon became active. The basalts that cap Steens Mountain, Abert Rim, and other ranges, unrelated contemporaries of the Columbia River flood basalts, erupted about 16 million years ago. Major faulting and uplift began in earnest less than 9 million years ago.

Steens Mountain, rising to 9,774 feet above the Alvord Desert, is a major Basin and Range escarpment. Hot springs mark the Alvord fault, one of the tension gashes across southeast Oregon that stretch the continent westward. In about 9 million years, the summit of Steens Mountain was uplifted 7,000 feet. While this seems like a lot of uplift, it works out to 9 inches per 1,000 years, or the equivalent of one magnitude 7 earthquake

View into Big Indian Gorge, Steens Mountain

TECTONIC ROTATION AND THE BASIN AND RANGE

If you'd like to invest in real estate and know that your holdings will automatically grow each year, then buy property at Plush or Adel, Frenchglen or Fields. For in remote southeast Oregon, where there seems to be plenty of landscape for everyone, the continent is stretching. In the Basin and Range, a restless mantle is forcing the earth's crust to expand east to west. Which it has, at about the rate a fingernail grows, for about the last 20 million years.

The stretching crust of the Basin and Range has shoved some parts of Oregon aside. In particular, it has rotated the Cascades, Klamath Mountains, and Coast Range to the west. This same stress has pulled the Blue Mountains northward as well, wrinkling the Columbia River basalts in the process. The tilted and thrust-faulted basalt flows near Mosier and The Dalles are the result of this motion. Altogether, the Coast and Klamaths have rotated some 20 degrees outward in the last 20 million years.

Tiny holes in these rocks show where cores were removed to measure the rotation and movement of the Hells Canyon terranes.

GEOLOGIC TIMETABLE 8: THE BASIN AND RANGE

Five significant events that shaped the landscape

Millions of years ago	Geologic era	Geologic event
0.000004 (4 years ago)	Holocene	Two magnitude 6 earthquakes strike Klamath Falls at the west margin of the Basin and Range in July 1993
14–present	Miocene to Holocene	Extensional faulting creates basins and ranges, including Steens Mountain, Abert Rim, Hart Mountain, and Alvord Desert
16	Miocene	Basalts that rim Steens Mountain erupt rapidly during a reversal of the earth's magnetic field
20–25	Miocene to Oligocene	Steens Mountain's volcanics, mostly andesite and rhyolite, erupt
225–300	Triassic to Paleozoic	Rocks exposed in the Pueblo Mountains formed

per 1,000 years. Not as earthshaking as it first seems. For 9 million years, the Basin and Range has been pulling apart, leaving fragments of crust floating on the mantle like ice on a rolling spring sea. Mantle fluids—the young basalt flows of Jordan Craters and a hundred other nameless vents—have oozed to the surface as the crust thins.

The Pueblo Mountains lie only 20 miles south of Steens Mountain, but their geology predates that of their neighbor by 180 million years. The Pueblos are also a product of Basin and Range faulting, but their core is hewn from the ancient rocks of an exotic terrane called the Sonoma. This terrane is composed of 200-million-year-old metamorphosed Jurassic volcanic and sedimentary rocks that once formed a chain of islands off the North American coastline and was added to the continent some 100 million years ago. These old rocks, exposed mostly in Nevada, are only remote cousins of the terranes in the Blue Mountains and the Klamaths.

On top of these old rocks, a complexity of Oligocene and Miocene volcanic rocks, including Steens volcanics and Steens basalts, compose much of the high country. The Pueblo caldera, which today is buried beneath the faulted valley east of the Pueblo Mountains, erupted 15.8 million years ago, immediately after the eruption of the Steens basalts, but only 500,000 years before the Mahogany Mountain and Three Fingers calderas in the Owyhees.

Exposed on the east face of the Pueblos are soft tuffs and late Miocene stream sediments that filled the caldera and were then uplifted by Basin and Range faulting during the last 10 million years.

Spaces here are open; trails are rare. One option is to follow old roads, animal trails, or the Desert Trail. On this broad avenue, there is no dusty rut to follow, only your own mind. The Desert Trail, a broadly defined

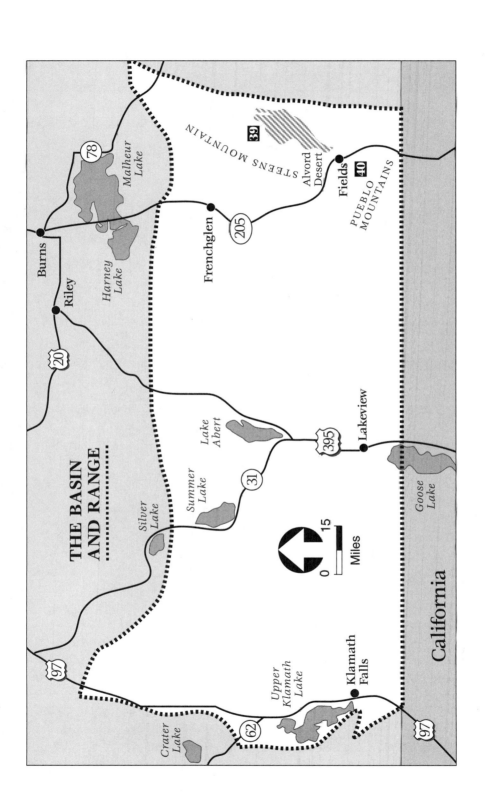

corridor on public land from Nevada to the Malheur National Forest in Oregon, traverses part of the Basin and Range. The hikes in this chapter serve as introductions to geology and landscapes in the few places where trails guide you. After that, take a map, water, and your imagination and just go.

STEENS MOUNTAIN RIM WALK

THE EDGE OF A FAULT BLOCK

Follow the rim of Steens Mountain from Wildhorse Lake to Kiger Gorge on informal paths.

DISTANCE ■ 12 miles one way

ELEVATION ■ 8,400 to 9,774 feet

DIFFICULTY ■ Moderate to strenuous

TOPOGRAPHIC MAPS ■ Wildhorse Lake, Alvord Hot Springs, Mann Lake, Big Pasture Creek; Steens Mountain Recreation Lands, BLM

GEOLOGIC MAPS ■ 39–42

PRECAUTIONS ■ The summit of Steens Mountain can attract and hold severe weather year-round; be prepared for snow, rain, high wind, and/or intense heat. There is no water on this route; carry plenty. The Steens Mountain Loop Road is open from July 1 to October 31; best time to try this hike is usually from July 15 to September 15. The hike can be done using a shuttle vehicle at the Kiger Gorge viewpoint.

FOR INFORMATION ■ Burns Bureau of Land Management office

About the Landscape: Steens Mountain, a two-decked layer cake of rock, is uplifted along the Alvord fault. Steens Mountain stands high above the desert not because it was built by lava flows, but because faults and earthquakes uplifted its east side long after the eruptions ceased.

The oldest rocks of Steens Mountain are the 20- to 25-million-year-old light-colored rocks exposed in its base. They jut from the Alvord Creek drainage, form the bottom of Devine Rock, and are best exposed along the eastern face of Steens. These rhyolites, dacites, and lakebed sediments (known as the Alvord Creek Formation, Pike Creek Formation, and Steens Mountain Volcanics) formed a low-slung complex of domes, andesites, stubby rhyolite flows, and thick layers of tuff. The sediments of small lakes reveal plant fossils of early Miocene age. The older rhyolites and andesites brought mineralization and ores with them. Gold, silver, and

Vesicles (holes produced by gas bubbles) and clustered feldspar crystals are visible in this piece of Steens basalt.

mercury have been mined from these rocks, especially where they are well exposed south of Steens Mountain.

The dark flows of Steens basalt form the top two-thirds of Steens Mountain's escarpment. Steens erupted rapidly about 16.2 million years ago; most basalt flows welled to the surface and then spread. The Steens basalts are flood basalts that erupted from fissures; the roots of these fissures are exposed as vertical dikes in the mountain's steep face. The Steens basalts appeared during a reversal of the earth's magnetic field. The changing direction of magnetic north and south are preserved in one single flow, about halfway down Steens Mountain's face. Many basalts on Steens Mountain bear interesting textures. Near Wildhorse Lake and elsewhere, basalt outcrops and boulders sport large rectangular white or gray crystals of *feldspar.* They often cluster in clumps, prompting the informal name turkey-track basalts for rocks with this distinctive texture. Other basalts display rounded holes, both large and small, which are the bubbles created by gas trapped in the cooling basalt lava.

The spectacular canyons of Steens Mountain were carved by glaciers. Big Indian, Kiger, and Blitzen Gorges display classic broad-bottomed U shapes. Wildhorse and Little Wildhorse Lakes are glacial cirques. During the Pleistocene, Steens Mountain sported an extensive ice cap. Glacial moraine extends 10 miles down Steens' gentle west slope. Polished and striated (scratched) bedrock surfaces are abundant from Fish Lake to the summit of Steens Mountain.

Trail Guide: Most people drive to the top of Steens Mountain on the new road, peer over the rim, express some degree of awe or humility, and drive away, thinking they've seen the place. And they have seen some of it. But they have not felt Steens Mountain, not breathed its wind, felt its heat, or touched its brooding, basaltic heart. This hike covers the descent to Wildhorse Lake and back, then walks along the rim of Steens Mountain to Kiger Gorge, examining rocks and landscape along the way. There is no developed trail; you can make the hike longer or shorter. Or you may drop a vehicle at Kiger Gorge, the farthest point on the hike, and drive back to the Wildhorse Lake trailhead. No developed trails connect the top and bottom of Steens Mountain, although the Desert Trail route extends from Frog Springs up along ridges above Wildhorse Canyon to the Wildhorse Lake parking lot.

To reach the trailhead at Wildhorse Lake, from Burns take US 20 east to Highway 205. Drive 75 miles south on Highway 205 to Frenchglen. From Frenchglen, take the Steens Mountain Loop Road 25 miles to the summit of Steens Mountain. From the summit, continue south to Wildhorse Lake trailhead.

Begin at the Wildhorse Lake and Steens Summit parking area at the end of Steens Mountain Road. You may wish to hike the 1-mile round-trip trail to the summit first for a breathtaking view (literally, at 9,774 feet). The 3-mile round-trip trail from the parking area down to Wildhorse Lake and back, while an undeveloped path, is easy to follow and the only trail to be found on the top of Steens Mountain. This small, turquoise lake is tucked into austere basaltic surroundings.

Ascend back to the parking area, and head upslope to the rim of Steens Mountain. There is no trail along the rim. However, the view from the top changes at every promontory and every canyon. At the south end of this walk, look for the older, lighter-colored volcanic rocks beneath the Steens basalts. Toward the developed East Rim overlook parking area, 2 miles north, feeder dikes of Steens basalt become more abundant. These vertical forms contrast markedly with the horizontal pancake-stack of basalt flows that compose the mountain. Many dikes create a linear spine. Dikes also cut through the headwall of Kiger Gorge and the narrow divide between Kiger Gorge and the east face of Steens Mountain.

This walk ends at the Kiger Gorge viewpoint, about 0.25 mile north of the main Steens Mountain loop road. This vista showcases a classic U-shaped glacial valley. Glacial polish has smoothed the outcrops at the head of Kiger Gorge. When you have had all the views, wind, cold, or heat you can handle, return along the top of Steens Mountain, or shuttle back to the Wildhorse Lake parking area.

Hike 40

ARIZONA CREEK TO STERGEN MEADOWS

ANCIENT ROCKS OF THE PUEBLO MOUNTAINS

Explore outcrops of Jurassic volcanos and reefs.

DISTANCE ■ 9 miles round trip

ELEVATION ■ 4,300 to 7,200 feet

DIFFICULTY ■ Moderate

TOPOGRAPHIC MAPS ■ Ladycomb Peak and Van Horn Basin

GEOLOGIC MAP ■ 43

PRECAUTIONS ■ Carry water. Watch out for rattlesnakes. The weather is capricious; be prepared for extreme heat, violent thunderstorms, and summer snow. Portions of the road are impassable when wet.

FOR INFORMATION ■ Burns Bureau of Land Management office

About the Landscape: The ancient rocks along Arizona Creek are mostly rhyolites, although there are a few fine-grained sedimentary rocks and limestones. All have been metamorphosed, and some, like many old rocks of the Pueblos, display the distinctive yellowish green that indicates the presence of the metamorphic mineral epidote. Many of the rhyolites are in the form of breccia—rocks broken by explosive eruptions or the high pressure of volcanic gases. Breccia is often a clue to the existence of minerals deposited by volcanic fluids; note the many mine pits that dot this area.

Trail Guide: To reach the trailhead, from Fields take Highway 205 south for 9.2 miles to Arizona Creek Road (BLM Road 82551-1-A0). Follow this unmarked dirt track east for 0.5 miles until you reach the BLM Wilderness Study Area sign at the mouth of Arizona Creek canyon. The hike begins here and follows the road for the first 1.5 miles, rising through soft

Rhyolite outcrops loom above Arizona Creek

slopes cut into the young Miocene gravels and tuffs. The bedding is best exposed in the slopes south of the road and in several steep exposures just above it.

About 1 mile up the canyon, a track veers upslope to the right. This path leads, in another mile, to several abandoned mines and glory holes (open pits) in the Jurassic rocks and to a fine view of the valley to the west. Return to the main road and continue to the crossing of Arizona Creek. The road continues left, switchbacking up Pueblo Mountain; follow the path straight ahead instead. This hiker's trail/cow path leads, in 2.5 miles, to inviting pinnacles and jagged outcrops of Jurassic rhyolite. Detailed examination of these rocks, and the talus along the trail, reveals the characteristic angular *clasts* (fragments) of volcanic breccia and, in the darker rocks, the yellow-green of epidote.

Above the pinnacles the trail meets a jeep track. Continue along the path through outcrops of metamorphosed rhyolite along the creek. About 3.5 miles into the walk, emerge from the canyon and note that the bedrock changes. From here to its end in Stergen Meadows, at 4.5 miles, the hike traverses Miocene Steens basalts and slightly older ash flow tuffs. Ambitious hikers may wish to scale the back side of Pueblo Mountain. Return the same way you came.

Chapter 9.
THE OWYHEES

Wind-sculpted and water-eroded tuffs, Leslie Gulch (Photo: Phil Bullock)

The Owyhees are tucked absent-mindedly into Oregon's back pocket like a rumpled dollar bill. Many dusty roads, but few trails, navigate their wrinkled landscape. Few hikers explore their canyons. The Owyhees remain a faraway, forgotten desert landscape, whose loudest voice is silence.

The Owyhees are the domain of *calderas*—flat-lying, explosive volcanos that produced ash and gas and gold. Owyhee geology is distinct from the High Lava Plains or the Basin and Range, although the rocks are similar in age.

The volcanos of the Owyhees first erupted 17 to 15 million years ago. Mahogany Mountain and Three Fingers Rock represent two of these old volcanos. The principal products of these two major calderas were gas and ash and explosive eruptions of hot, thick, sticky ash-flow tuffs. Today these rocks form the cliffs of Leslie Gulch and Succor Creek.

The second period of geologic activity followed closely on the heels of

CALDERAS

The term *caldera* has several meanings. Its most common use describes the large crater in the summit of a volcano that forms by collapse after an explosive eruption. Crater Lake, the caldera at Mauna Loa, and the summit crater of Newberry Volcano are good examples of these.

The term also refers to another phenomenon, common in the Owyhees of southeast Oregon, the caldera volcano. These rank among the world's largest and least visible volcanos. This kind of volcano explosively erupts huge volumes of ash and rhyolite. The eruptions empty the magma chamber, resulting in the collapse of the surface. This collapse occurs along semicircular ring fractures (a scenario similar to what occurred at Crater Lake). As the volcano's roof collapses, violent eruptions jet from the fractures. After the collapse, additional rhyolite and/or basalt often builds a dome or cinder cone in the volcano's center.

Calderas of this type are associated with gold deposits in southeast Oregon and northwest Nevada. The calderas of the Owyhees erupted about 10 million years ago. Several, including Grassy Mountain and Mahogany Mountain, are the focus of gold prospectors and mining.

GEOLOGIC TIMETABLE 9: THE OWYHEES

Five significant events that shaped the landscape

Millions of years ago	Geologic era	Geologic event
2–3	Pliocene	Regional tilting drains Lake Idaho northward, changes the course of the Snake River, and begins carving Hells Canyon
7	Miocene	Large lake (Lake Idaho) fed by Snake River occupies much of the northern Owyhees and Snake River Plain
10–14	Miocene	Epithermal gold deposits form as extensional faulting opens an extensive north–south graben
15.5	Miocene	Three Fingers caldera erupts depositing Spring Creek tuff and tuffs exposed along Succor Creek
15.8	Miocene	Caldera at Mahogany Mountain erupts, creating Leslie Gulch tuff

the calderas. The scene of action shifted west. From 14.5 to about 12 million years ago, the central part of the Owyhees began to pull apart, forming a north–south fault-bounded valley (the Oregon–Idaho graben) that today extends through the town of Harper. Parts of this valley contained lakes. Volcanic eruptions poured into these shallow lakes, producing layered ash and pillow basalts.

The third period of volcanic activity persisted from 10 to about 6 million years ago. The spotlight shifted west again. Several large volcanic centers, including Saddle Mountain, Star Butte, and Mustang Butte, erupted. Basalts and rhyolites poured out of these rhyolite volcanos.

As these eruptions dwindled, a new chapter in Owyhee geologic history began. Faulting created a broad valley. Water from the southward-draining Snake River collected in a deepening valley, creating a lake. This lake, called Lake Idaho, persisted from about 7 until 2 million years ago. The fragile sedimentary rocks of this lakebed stand as stark white cliffs north of Harper. About 2 million years ago, broad regional tilting drained Lake Idaho and helped create the present northward course of the Snake River.

The last eruptive episode lasted from about 2 million until only 4,000 years ago. These relatively young lavas include the flows at Jordan Craters (about 4,000 years in age) and the basalts that surround Saddle Butte (about 100,000 years old).

Today, the Owyhees are best known for their no-see-um gold deposits: the gold in Owyhee rocks is so fine-grained that it cannot be recognized with the naked eye, a hand lens, or even a microscope. These extremely

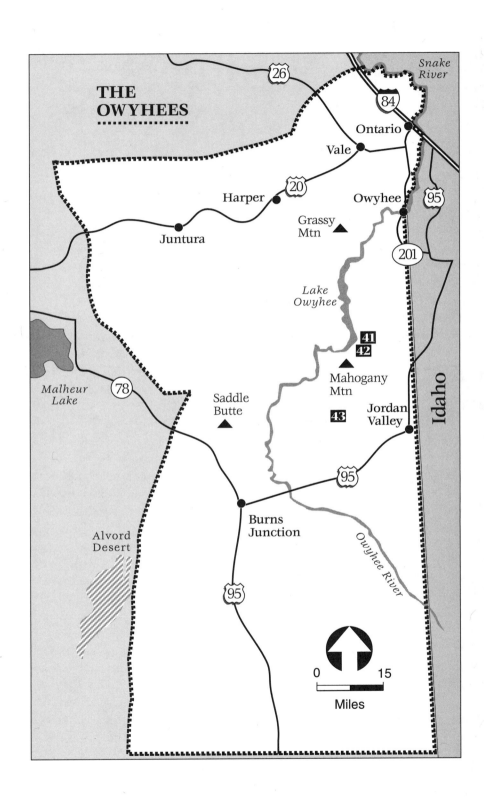

THE
OWYHEES

Snake
River

26

84

Ontario

Vale

20

Harper

Owyhee

95

Juntura

Grassy
Mtn

201

Lake
Owyhee

41
42

Malheur
Lake

78

Saddle
Butte

Mahogany
Mtn

43

Jordan
Valley

Idaho

95

Alvord
Desert

Burns
Junction

Owyhee River

95

0   15

Miles

fine-grained gold deposits are created when hot, acid water circulates through rhyolites, dissolving gold on their way. When this water surfaces and boils at hot springs, it deposits the gold. The Grassy Mountain gold deposit is the best known in the Owyhees. Epithermal gold is commonly mined in an open pit, and the gold is extracted using a controversial cyanide leaching process.

THREE FINGERS GULCH

Hike

41

AN ANCIENT COLLAPSED CALDERA

Trek to one of the oldest and best exposed—and one of the most accessible—caldera complexes in the Owyhees.

DISTANCE ■ 5 miles one way

ELEVATION ■ 2,700 to 3,800 feet

DIFFICULTY ■ Strenuous

TOPOGRAPHIC MAPS ■ Pelican Point, Bannock Ridge, Rooster Comb

GEOLOGIC MAPS ■ 44, 45, 50, 51

PRECAUTIONS ■ Summer weather is torrid and dehydration is a serious threat; take twice the water you would in the mountains. Rattlesnakes abound; be watchful and remember that a calm but rapid retreat is the safest way to deal with a snake. Roads are muddy to the point of impassability in the early spring (March) and in wet weather.

FOR INFORMATION ■ Vale Bureau of Land Management office

About the Landscape: Three Fingers Caldera is one of the largest and oldest eruptive complexes in the Owyhees. This huge, low-slung volcano erupted explosively 15.5 million years ago. It produced the rhyolites along Succor Creek Road and the multicolored ash-flow tuff formation of Leslie Gulch. Three Fingers Gulch exposes the dramatic geology of the caldera rim—mostly rhyolite dikes that slash through multicolored tuffs.

Trail Guide: This hike takes you into Three Fingers Gulch for a view of the ancient collapsed rim and interior of the old caldera. The hike follows jeep trails and Three Fingers Creek, because there are no developed hiking trails. Three Fingers Rock is perched at the east rim of Three Fingers Gulch between Succor Creek and Lake Owyhee.

From Ontario, drive south on US 26/20 to Highway 201. Continue south on Highway 201 past Adrian. Turn right on Succor Creek Road. Succor Creek Road winds through red- and tan-colored rhyolites that erupted from Three Fingers Caldera. Follow Succor Creek Road approximately 20 miles

Cliffs formed from the tuffs erupted from the Mahogany Mountain caldera

to Leslie Gulch Road. Turn west on Leslie Gulch Road. Approximately 3.8 miles along Leslie Gulch Road, a narrow gravel road (Long Gulch Road) turns sharply north. Follow this road 4.25 miles to a narrow saddle between Long Gulch and Three Fingers Creek. Park on this saddle. Follow a steep jeep trail downslope into Three Fingers Gulch.

This rough, steep road takes you to the bottom of Three Fingers Gulch in a walk of about 2.5 miles. At the bottom, follow the creek bottom downstream about 1 mile until you are cliffed out by a steep precipice above

Owyhee Reservoir. Upstream from the road, you can follow the streambed for at least 2 miles for spectacular views of the caldera's rim and inner walls.

The walk to the bottom of Three Fingers Gulch follows an old fault. The canyon walls expose the Leslie Gulch ash-flow tuff. This thick unit erupted from Mahogany Mountain—a large caldera to the south. The Leslie Gulch tuff here varies from 250 to 1,000 feet thick. It displays thin, wavy, glassy clasts (called *fiamme*).

On the north wall of Three Fingers Creek, dikes that intruded the caldera rim before its collapse are visible along the canyon wall. On the south side of the canyon, softer, light-colored sedimentary rocks are exposed. Most of these rocks are composed of silt and volcanic ash (tuff). These rocks may once have filled a moat—a down-faulted ring along the outer edge of the collapsed caldera wall. After exploring the canyon, return as you came.

Hike 42

LESLIE GULCH

COLORFUL CANYONS OF A CALDERA

Several side trips up rugged side canyons bring you closer to the multicolored Leslie Gulch tuff.

DISTANCE ■ 2–3.5 miles one way

ELEVATION ■ 3,100 to 3,600 feet

DIFFICULTY ■ Moderate

TOPOGRAPHIC MAP ■ Rooster Comb

GEOLOGIC MAPS ■ 46, 50

PRECAUTIONS ■ Summer weather is torrid and dehydration is a serious threat; take twice the water you would in the mountains. Rattlesnakes abound; be watchful and remember that a calm, quick retreat is the safest way to deal with a snake. Roads are muddy to the point of impassability in the early spring (March) and in wet weather.

FOR INFORMATION ■ Vale Bureau of Land Management office

About the Landscape: The tawny, 15.5-million-year-old rocks of Leslie Gulch erupted from the Mahogany Mountain caldera just to the south. This caldera is the oldest in the Owyhees. Part of the vast caldera vent system is exposed about 7 miles down the Leslie Gulch Road, near the cabin at Mud Spring (Diablo Canyon); dark red rhyolite dikes that carried lavas to the surface cut through the tawny canyon walls. The Leslie Gulch ash-flow tuff was only one product of the Mahogany Mountain caldera's eruption.

Spires in Leslie Gulch tuffs (Photo: Phil Bullock)

Ash from this volcano covered thousands of square miles. A variety of rhyolite domes and flows also scatter across the landscape here. By 14.9 million years ago, the caldera quieted and eruptions from the main vent complex ceased.

Trail Guide: The most scenic route to Leslie Gulch Road begins in Idaho. Take US 95 south from I-84. Two miles after US 95 crosses into Oregon, turn west on Succor Creek Road. Follow Succor Creek Road west and north 6 miles and turn west onto the broad, inviting surface of Leslie Gulch Road. After 7 miles, Upper Leslie Gulch canyon opens to the south. It is marked only by a small informal turnout on the south side of the road.

The informal trail fades after the first 0.5 mile, but the open canyon is easily navigated on animal trails. Cavities in the tan to yellow Leslie Gulch tuffs were created by gas bubbles; a few are the casts of other rocks carried along in the powerful ash flow. In about 2 miles, reach Upper Leslie

Gulch, which leads to Mahogany Mountain—the source of the Leslie Gulch ash-flow tuff that dominates the landscape here. When you've gone as far as you'd like, retrace your steps back down the gulch.

JORDAN CRATERS

Hike
43

ROPY YOUNG BASALTS AT COFFEEPOT CRATER

This 4,000-year-old sea of basaltic lava looks as though it erupted yesterday.

DISTANCE ■ 1 mile or more

ELEVATION ■ 3,500 feet

DIFFICULTY ■ Easy to moderate

TOPOGRAPHIC MAPS ■ Jordan Craters North, Jordan Craters South

GEOLOGIC MAPS ■ 48–50

PRECAUTIONS ■ The drive to isolated Jordan Craters is long, but well worth the bumps. Parts of this road can be muddy. This area is torrid in the summer; the trip is best attempted in May or September. No services after US 95.

FOR INFORMATION ■ Vale Bureau of Land Management office

About the Landscape: Jordan Craters are among the youngest and youngest-looking basalts in Oregon. They are part of a group of basalt cones, including nearby Clarks Butte and Rocky Butte, that erupted a very fluid alkali olivine basalt lava. Jordan Craters erupted 4,000 years ago.

The ropy *pahoehoe* textures of Jordan Craters basalts contrast with rubbly *aa* lavas common in the Cascades. The smooth flows from Jordan Craters belie their rugged topography. Collapse pits, small spatter cones, lava gutters, and lava tubes challenge the cross-country hiker.

Trail Guide: From I-84 in Idaho, take US 95 south about 60 miles. Turn west on Jordan Craters Road, about 2 miles past an old school house. Drive west a total of 35 miles on Jordan Craters Road which becomes Blow Out Reservoir Road. Jordan Craters' Lava Field becomes visible in the last 7 miles of the drive. As you pass most of the flow, the road curves and rises up a hill. An unmarked road to the left takes you to the Jordan Craters Lava Field, Coffeepot Crater, and the beginning of the hike.

From the parking lot, a 1-mile trail leads around Coffeepot Crater. It offers memorable views of the stratified lava flows inside this vent. Trace a counter-clockwise path around the loop to encounter a wonderland of lava flow forms. The *gutters*, or lava flow paths, as well as ropy *pahoehoe*

Grass and rabbitbrush prosper in a collapsed lava tube at Jordan Craters.

surfaces and thinly surfaced lava tubes, are plainly evident. The layers on the crater walls are built of successive flows. Continue around the crater to the cindered slope. The trail gains strength up this slope, and leads to another overview of Coffeepot Crater. From the top you can see the flow patterns of the basalt as it moved toward Cow Lakes. The spatter cones and hoodoos on the west side of the crater are classic examples of blow-outs, or cones built of spattered, hot, gooey lava bombs.

Chapter 10.
THE BLUE MOUNTAINS

A granite dike cuts through sedimentary rocks, Wallowa Mountains.

Before the Blue Mountains, there was no Oregon, and ocean waves broke on Idaho beaches. And if there were seaports in the Triassic, Cambridge and McCall would have been the cloistered towns of shipwrights and seafaring hunters of the ichthyosaur.

Geologically, the Blue Mountains stretch from Prineville to Hells Canyon and include the Ochoco, Strawberry, Elkhorn, and Wallowa ranges. They are defined by the presence of the ancient rocks of a tropical island arc system, and the persistence of a broad structural upwarp known as the Blue Mountains anticline. The eastern and central Blue Mountains best display the rocks of ancient islands. The western Blue Mountains showcase younger volcanic rocks that knit the islands to North America.

THE EASTERN BLUE MOUNTAINS

On a snowy August day in the Wallowas, it is hard to realize you are walking in what once was a tropical sea. Yet with a little imagination, you can be in Tahiti. For the Wallowa Mountains' rocks, like those of neighboring Hells Canyon, originated as reef-fringed volcanic South Sea islands—about the latitude of modern Hawaii. Hells Canyon is carved from the volcanos; the Wallowa Mountains feature coral reefs and the adjacent seafloor. The seafloor in the Wallowa Mountains combined with volcanic rocks in Hells Canyon compose the Wallowa terrane.

Hells Canyon displays the twisted wreckage of ancient volcanos. Like a double-decker bus, there are two generations of volcanos here, one built atop the other. The oldest volcanos (275 million years in age, or Permian) stretch along the Snake River from Oxbow north to Hells Canyon Dam. The tattered remnants of younger (Triassic) rocks extend from the dam north to Asotin, Washington. All these volcanic rocks—originally andesite and basalt—bear the greenish hue of age and abuse. They have been altered to greenstone, a low-temperature metamorphic rock. In the Wallowa Mountains, more green-hued volcanic rocks frame the Wallowa River, proving the link between Hells Canyon and the Wallowas.

Most of the Wallowa Mountains' layered rocks are coral reefs and sediments that fringed and ultimately covered the island volcanos. Some 200 million years ago, tropical fish swam at Sacajewea Peak and ichthyosaurs played on its flanks. The soft gray limestone of Sacajewea Peak, Marble Mountain, and Hurwall and Hurricane Divides was a flourishing coral reef complex. Today the rocks preserve a fossil ecosystem of clams, brachiopods, corals, and sponges. Some of these fossils bear striking resemblance to fossils of similar age from Asia and the Swiss Alps, establishing a tenuous link to Asia in this exotic terrane.

The partial skeleton of an ichthyosaur, a marine reptile that was a relative

GEOLOGIC TIMETABLE 10: THE BLUE MOUNTAINS

Five significant events that shaped the landscape

Millions of years ago	Geologic era	Geologic event
0.010–1.6	Pleistocene	Glaciers carve mountain tops; glacial sediments fill valleys
13–present	Miocene	Faulting on Olympic–Wallowa lineament uplifts mountains and downdrops valley floors
18–14	Miocene	Columbia River basalts erupt; Strawberry volcanics erupt
50–40	Eocene	Clarno volcanos erupt
400–100	Mesozoic and Paleozoic	Blue Mountain island arc forms, dies, collides with the continent, and becomes the new western edge of North America

of dinosaurs and looked like a porpoise, was found at the formation's *type locality* (the place the formation was first described and named) at Martin's Bridge on Eagle Creek. It is one of the few dinosaur relatives found in eastern Oregon's rocks. Because this region was a series of small islands far from a major landmass during most of the Mesozoic, four-footed dinosaurs never roamed the ancient, tropical beaches of the Eastern Blue Mountains.

Hard, white rock cores the Wallowa Mountains from Eagle Cap to Cornucopia to Minam Lake. These rocks look like granite, feel like granite, and break like granite. But they are not granite. Though they are similar, subtle differences in minerals and chemical compositions distinguish them from classic granites. Geologists call the rocks of the Wallowa batholith *granitic rocks.* The most abundant are granodiorite and tonalite. These bland white rocks provided Oregon's richest and longest-lasting gold mine, at Cornucopia.

The Columbia River basalts cap the Wallowa terrane. The layered slopes of the Imnaha River canyon and the upper ramparts of Hells Canyon, as well as the tops of several Wallowa Mountain peaks, are Columbia River basalt.

The Wallowa Mountains have been uplifted more than 7,000 feet by the Wallowa fault (and other faults on the south and west sides of the range). Faulting began about 13 million years ago and still uplifts the range today.

The Wallowa's most recent chapter was written by glaciers. Nine major glaciers chiseled the Wallows into their present form during the Pleistocene. Wallowa Lake, swaddled in gravelly moraine, is Oregon's second-deepest lake.

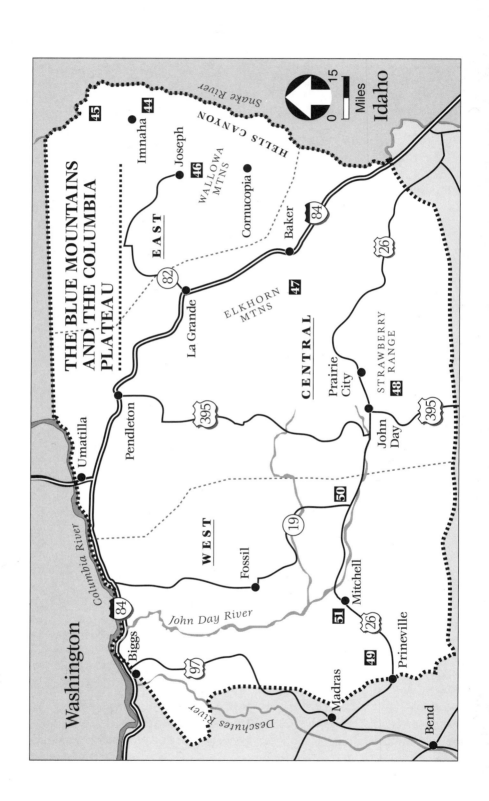

THE BLUE MOUNTAINS AND THE COLUMBIA PLATEAU

Washington

Idaho

0   15
Miles

Snake River

HELLS CANYON

45

Imnaha

44

Joseph

46

WALLOWA MTNS

Cornucopia

EAST

Baker

84

82

26

La Grande

ELKHORN MTNS

47

CENTRAL

Prairie City

STRAWBERRY RANGE

48

395

Pendleton

395

Umatilla

John Day

Columbia River

50

WEST

19

Fossil

Mitchell

84

John Day River

51

26

Biggs

97

Madras

49

Prineville

Deschutes River

Bend

SNAKE RIVER AND TEMPERANCE CREEK TRAILS

HELLS CANYON

This very rigorous hike explores the oldest and youngest rocks of the Wallowa terrane.

DISTANCE ■ 44-mile loop

ELEVATION ■ 6,982 to 1,210 feet

DIFFICULTY ■ Strenuous

TOPOGRAPHIC MAPS ■ Old Timer Mountain, Hat Point, Kirkwood Creek, Temperance Creek, Sleepy Ridge, Graves Point, Lord Flat

GEOLOGIC MAPS ■ 52, 54

PRECAUTIONS ■ Allow at least 6 days for this rigorous hike. Carry ample water and water purification equipment. Watch for poison oak and poison ivy. The access road is normally open mid-May to mid-October, but note that on hot summer days temperatures in Hells Canyon may exceed 110 degrees. Portions of the trail may be in poor condition; some sections are bordered by a precipitous drop to the Snake River; proceed with caution beyond Temperance Creek.

FOR INFORMATION ■ Hells Canyon National Recreation Area

Publisher's note: Fires in 1996 caused extensive damage in this area; check with Hells Canyon National Recreation Area before attempting this hike.

About the Landscape: Hells Canyon is a volcanic layer cake. At its top, two generations of Columbia River basalt hover above the abyss: the upper cliffs are mostly Grande Ronde basalt, 15 million years old. The bench below this first steep drop is older Imnaha basalts, 17 to 18 million years in age and the first Columbia River basalt to erupt. They are found only in this corner of northeast Oregon.

Ancient volcanic rocks of the Wallowa terrane form the inner walls of Hells Canyon. The foundation of these ancient volcanos is the Cougar Creek complex, exposed along the Snake River at Cougar Creek. These rocks represent old oceanic crust and include the oldest known igneous rocks in northeast Oregon, a gabbro dated at 309 million years. The rocks here are stressed, stretched, and deformed. What was once a solid diorite has been transformed to flaky, fragile schist near Salt Creek. High metamorphic temperature and pressure have modified bland diorites into racing-striped, black-banded amphibolite.

Pittsburgh Landing you can rest by a pristine lake in a moist, magnolia-shaded glen between two great volcanos. Of course, to find this scene today you must look in the rocks. This is home of the Pittsburgh Landing Formation; 200 million years ago these soft sandstones and shales were deposited in shallow lakes between two volcanos. Still younger Jurassic rocks rest on the south side of Pittsburgh Landing. In 1996 the Salt Creek fire burned the entire area of this hike. Look for evidence of bunchgrass and shrub rejuvenation as well as places where "stand replacement" burns have destroyed Douglas-fir groves on the north slopes and ponderosa pine on the south slopes.

OREGON'S EARTHQUAKES

Several major fault systems threaten Oregon with earthquakes. Two different mechanisms are responsible. The most severe quake threat comes from a subduction-zone earthquake. Like the 1964 magnitude 9 Alaska earthquake, this threat arises from the movement of the ocean crust deep beneath the surface. Evidence from coastal marshes and beach terraces suggests that Oregon experiences one of these quakes every 300 to 400 years. The last such quake probably occurred about 1700.

The other major force that generates earthquakes is crustal extension. Following the example of California, much of Oregon is trying to move toward the northwest. This motion occurs on the Portland Hills fault, the Mount Angel fault near Woodburn, and in eastern Oregon on the many faults of the Olympic–Wallowa Lineament, known as the OWL. Other fault zones are also active in eastern Oregon.

The OWL stretches from the Wallowa Mountains to the Olympic Peninsula. Over the last 6 to 10 million years, its faults have uplifted the Wallowa Mountains more than 7,000 feet and uplifted Rattlesnake Mountain 3,000 feet above the Hanford Nuclear Reservation. Activity on OWL faults has rattled Halfway and Milton Freewater with magnitude 5 earthquakes.

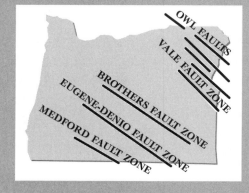

Greenstones line Hells Canyon.

Trail Guide: From Joseph, take County Road 350 east to Imnaha. From downtown Imnaha, drive east on USFS Road 4240 about 30 miles to Hat Point and Hat Point Campground.

Trail 1752 plunges off the Hat Point observation walkway and switchbacks into Hells Canyon. It crosses fine-grained Grande Ronde Columbia River basalts on these steep slopes. Trail 1752 joins trail 1751 at about 2 miles and 4,400 feet elevation, where the slope flattens onto a bench of Imnaha Columbia River basalts. Follow trail 1751 a short distance to trail 1748, which continues northward across the bench and into Hells Canyon. As trail 1748 dives off the bench, it leaves the Columbia River basalts and cuts its way across the dark, hard greenstones of the Blue Mountains island arc. They continue to the bottom of Hells Canyon, where trail 1748 meets the Snake River Trail (trail 1726) at Sluice Creek, about 5 miles from Hat Point and 5,620 feet lower. For the 2 miles downstream from Sluice Creek, campsites line the Snake River trail as it follows easy riverbanks.

In the next 7 miles to Temperance Creek, the Snake River trail edges along the river, in some places cut into the rock outcrops above the Snake. These rocks are Triassic greenstones, sediments, and mudflow deposits. At Temperance Creek, about 14 miles from Hat Point, there are a few good camping sites.

The 10 miles from Temperance Creek to Pittsburgh Landing are flat (but challenging for those uncomfortable on cliffs) as the Snake River trail follows the Cougar Creek complex, the highlight of this hike. These gabbros, greenstones, and amphibolites are the foundation of the Blue Mountain arc; 300 million years ago this was the ocean bottom. At Pittsburgh Landing good camping sites abound. The soft Jurassic shales at the south end of Pittsburgh Landing represent the youngest rocks of the Wallowa terrane. They contain tiny fragments of Idaho's Precambrian bedrock, certain evidence that North America was close at hand 150 million years ago. These are the youngest rocks of the Wallowa terrane, deposited just before the ancient arc docked with North America. Fossil leaves of oak, maple, and other hardwood trees occur in these rocks of the Coon Hollow Formation.

From Pittsburgh Landing, return the 10 miles along the Snake River trail to Temperance Creek. Take the Temperance Creek trail (trail 1778) upslope along Temperance Creek, which follows the contact between the Wallowa terrane's volcanic rocks on the south and the magma chambers that fed the volcanos (diorite) on the north. The trail rises across more Triassic volcanic rocks, including a wide variety of sediments and mudflow deposits. At 5 miles from the Snake River trail (trail 1726), at the intersection with trail 1751, 2,800 feet, is the Wisnor Place, an old homestead that makes a good campsite. This location is one of the few sites with water before the rigorous 15-mile uphill return climb to Hat Point; stock up on water here.

From the Wisnor Place, follow trail 1751 upslope to the south, across the older rocks and onto the Columbia River basalts. Trail 1751 follows this ridgetop and the basalt benches. It merges into a gradual—but very long—grade that continues for 13 miles all the way back to trail 1752, which crawls the final 2 miles steeply upslope to return to Hat Point.

NEE ME POO NATIONAL HISTORIC TRAIL

Hike 45

HELLS CANYON

View Imnaha basalt and the roots of island arc volcanos on a historic Native American trail.

DISTANCE ■ 14-mile loop

ELEVATION ■ 1,005 to 2,380 feet

DIFFICULTY ■ Moderate

TOPOGRAPHIC MAPS ■ Cactus Mountain, Dead Horse Ridge

GEOLOGIC MAPS ■ 52, 54

PRECAUTIONS ■ The unpaved portion of the Imnaha River Road is rough; it may be muddy and impassable for passenger cars in early spring (February to April); 4WD is strongly recommended. The road is narrow and curvy; use caution; allow at least 2 hours to drive from Joseph to the trailhead. The bottoms of the Imnaha and Hells Canyons are extremely hot during summer months, and commonly reach temperatures of 110 degrees; this hike is best during spring or fall. Poison oak and ivy infest the bottom of Hells Canyon. Rattlesnakes and prickly pear abound.

FOR INFORMATION ■ Hells Canyon National Recreation Area

About the Landscape: The Imnaha River has sliced its canyon through a layer cake of Columbia River basalts. The basalts at the bottom of this canyon are the oldest and most primitive, or mantle-like, Columbia River basalt and are known as the Imnaha basalt. These flows erupted about 17 to 18 million years ago. The Imnaha area was a lowland at that time, and many flows simply ponded here, filling the depression. The Imnaha flows do not cover a very wide area and are best exposed in this canyon. The large crystals evident in many of these dark flows are the hallmark of the Imnaha basalts.

The lower end of the Imnaha River cuts its gorge through an old magma chamber of the ancient arc. This hard, greenish white diorite forms rugged outcrops that are ideal habitat for Rocky Mountain sheep. This rock is 260 million years old, Permian in age. It fed the eruptions of the first generation of volcanos in the Wallowa terrane. Then, uplifted and eroded, it served as a solid foundation for the second generation of Wallowa terrane eruptions 40 million years later.

Similar rocks appear along the Snake River near Dug Bar and form the steep terrane along the Snake at the mouth of Deep Creek. At Deep Creek, the dark rocks are mostly gabbro. They are cross-cut by light-colored dikes

179

Columbia River basalts dominate much of the Nee Me Poo Trail to Dug Bar.

of rocks similar to granites. The age of the Deep Creek plutonic complex is 231 million years.

Trail Guide: This hike travels the Nee Me Poo Trail to the Snake River, then follows a road back for a loop trip. The Nee Me Poo Trail to Dug Bar follows the path of Chief Joseph's band as they fled their homeland in 1877, pursued by the US Cavalry. The Nez Perce, including women, children, the elderly, and all their livestock, forced from their homeland in the Wallowa Valley, followed this trail, crossed the Snake River at Dug Bar when the Snake was at its peak flow in mid-May, and fled toward Canada.

From Joseph, take County Road 350 to Imnaha. Turn north on Imnaha River Road. Follow this road to the end of pavement, and continue cautiously, going another 20 miles on gravel and dirt roads. Cross the Imnaha River and at the Cow Creek trailhead, follow the trail (which begins as a rough road that you can drive for the next 2.5 miles if you wish) to the right. (The left trail follows the Imnaha River through a canyon cut into the Imnaha pluton, an 8-mile round trip to Eureka Bar and the historic Eureka Mine on the Snake River.)

The road to the right climbs gradually out of the canyon and up the flank of Cactus Mountain. This road weaves along the contact of the Imnaha pluton and Columbia River basalt. At a weathered sign about 2.5 miles into the hike, the road intersects the Nee Me Poo (Nez Perce) National Trail. Follow this trail, which branches to the right, as it heads directly up the small canyon toward Lone Pine Saddle. The basalts here are Imnaha type, with large crystals of feldspar. Grande Ronde basalt appears at Lone Pine Saddle, and on Cactus Mountain immediately north.

From Lone Pine Saddle, the Nee Me Poo Trail drops through Columbia River basalts to the Snake River at Dug Bar. There are opportunities to camp along the river. Two miles to the south, rugged topography along the Snake displays the Deep Creek pluton, a magma chamber of the old island arc. Only informal trails provide access to the steep terrain.

To return to the trailhead from Dug Bar, follow the road north along the river. This part of the hike encounters older, highly deformed rocks before turning upslope and returning through basalts to the trailhead at Cow Creek, 8 miles from Dug Bar.

LAKES BASIN AND EAGLE CAP

Hike 46

WALLOWA MOUNTAINS

Cover some of northeast Oregon's most serene landscape: granites and ancient seafloor exposed in the Wallowa Mountains.

DISTANCE ■ 18.5 miles one way

ELEVATION ■ 5,100 to 7,600 feet

DIFFICULTY ■ Moderate

TOPOGRAPHIC MAPS ■ Eagle Cap, Chief Joseph Mountain, North Minam Meadows; Eagle Cap Wilderness map (from Geographics, Eugene)

GEOLOGIC MAPS ■ 53, 54

PRECAUTIONS ■ Beware of ravenous mosquitoes. This hike requires a shuttle vehicle. Inquire at Eagle Cap Ranger District about restrictions on availability of campsites, number of campers, and length of stay.

FOR INFORMATION ■ Eagle Cap Ranger District

About the Landscape: The core of the Wallowa Mountains is granitic rock. Altogether, twelve separate intrusions comprise the Wallowa batholith. Most are similar in appearance and age—about 145 to 160 million years. These rocks are mostly tonalite and granodiorite. The black, iron-rich minerals in these rocks are mostly *hornblende*—a hard, prismatic or rectangular mineral. *Biotite*—a flaky, soft, dark brown mica—is less abundant.

Although granites in Oregon are often associated with gold deposits, the Wallowas are notoriously gold-poor. This paucity of precious metal is probably due to the surrounding sedimentary rocks which, as former coral reefs and shallow seafloor, had little gold to share with the invading granitic magmas. The sole exception is the Cornucopia Stock, at the southeast edge of the Wallowas. Cornucopia hosted Oregon's largest lode gold mine, which operated until 1948.

The heat of the Wallowa batholith recrystallized the surrounding sedimentary rocks. The Martin Bridge limestone displays the most radically altered textures. The heat of the adjacent intrusion transformed the limestone into a sugary, granular marble.

Trail Guide: To drop a shuttle vehicle at the hike's end, from Joseph take the Hurricane Creek Road. Drive 8 miles west to the road's end. Leave the vehicle in the parking lot at the Hurricane Creek trailhead. To reach the Two Pan trailhead at the hike's beginning, from Joseph take Highway 82 west to Lostine. Turn south on Lostine River Road. After approximately 5 miles the road changes to USFS Road 8210. Two Pan trailhead is at road's end, approximately 15 miles south of Lostine. This road is maintained and passable for passenger cars, but becomes narrow and rough for the last 6 miles beyond Lostine Guard Station.

From the parking lot for Two Pan campground, take trail 1662 along the East Fork of the Lostine River. This trail is rough and eroded for the first 2 miles. It climbs steeply through a forest of Englemann spruce and western larch (tamarack), emerging into meadows with a good view of Hurricane Divide towering to the east. The layered rocks of Hurricane Divide are sedimentary rocks of the Hurwall Formation; gray Martin Bridge limestone forms the base of cliffs. At 3 miles the trail enters a long meadow with an enticing view of Eagle Cap, one of the highest peaks of the Wallowas, rising at the end. The trail follows the flat meadow's west side. Outcrops along the way showcase details of the Wallowa batholith; at about 3.5 miles, fine-grained pinkish white dikes in flat-lying exposures just west of the trail inlay rectangular designs on glacially polished bedrock; dark, rounded clots of older rock (the Hurwal Formation), wedged from the intrusion's sides and roof and marinated for a million years in liquid granite, blend into the surrounding white stone.

As lodgepole pine and alpine fir forest close in on the south end of the valley, the trail resumes switchbacking to the upper Lakes Basin. It abruptly disgorges the hiker at 7.3 miles into the elongate, glacially

Eagle Cap rises above Lakes Basin.

sculpted Lakes Basin at the foot of Eagle Cap. Camping spots are at a premium here. The best tent sites are away from the major valley and trail area—and must be more than 100 feet away from water.

In the Lakes Basin, Eagle Cap dominates the landscape. Its white rock is granodiorite. Columbia River basalt dikes form red streaks through its sides and summit. The Lakes Basin served as a central area for the Wallowa Ice Cap of the Pleistocene. From this basin, glaciers radiated across the range. Three major drainages—the Lostine River, Hurricane Creek, and the Wallowa River—all originate from near Mirror Lake, the first major lake that the trail encounters.

To complete the hike from Lakes Basin, take trail 1807 to Hurricane Creek. The gray limestone (now marble) peaks of Sacajewea and Matterhorn loom ahead on the east side of the valley. The trip down Hurricane Creek provides superb but remote views of the dark reddish brown Hurwal Formation on the upper part of Hurwal Divide, and the solemn gray of the Martin Bridge limestone (here, marble). The Martin

Folds are visible in marble metamorphosed from limestone along the Hurricane Creek trail.

Bridge Formation represents shallow warm waters that surrounded the old volcanos. The darker Hurwal represents shales deposited above the limestone as the volcanos sank, the water deepened, and the island arc moved northward.

White streaks across the upper parts of the ridge are granitic dikes— the fingers of the Wallowa batholith or the Sawtooth Stock to the north grasping the adjacent country rock. At 5.1 miles from Lakes Basin, inviting camping sites occur along Hurricane Creek meadows near the junction with the Echo Lake Trail (trail 1824).

At Slick Rock Creek, 2.5 miles from Hurricane Creek meadows, a large, red-brown dike of Columbia River basalt (Imnaha basalt) slices across the stream just upslope from the trail. West of the trail, the thin red spires atop the summit of Twin Peaks are Imnaha basalt—perhaps the flow fed by this dike. Mountain goats patrol the slopes of Hurricane Divide, and may be seen trekking across these slopes in the late afternoon. At Falls Creek, 1.5 miles from Slick Rock Creek, a superb outcrop of folded Martin Bridge limestone gives a great excuse for a refreshing pause before hiking the last mile to the Hurricane Creek trailhead. In this last wilderness mile, much of the forest has been clear-cut—not by loggers, but by winter avalanches and torrential spring storms.

THE CENTRAL BLUE MOUNTAINS

Most of the central Blue Mountains, from the Elkhorn Mountains west to the Strawberry Mountains and Mitchell, are floored by chaos. Geologists call it the Baker terrane. This terrane represents ocean-floor rocks and the subduction zone that carried the seafloor down beneath the island arc volcanos. The old rocks of the Baker terrane are thoroughly deformed and scrambled. Mapping geology in the Baker terrane is like mapping a teenager's closet.

This disordered collection of rocks is called a *melange*—French for "mixture." In the Baker terrane, Permian rocks lie adjacent to Triassic; Devonian limestones rest against Triassic basalt. The melange resembles a stew—a carrot here, a potato there. The matrix of this geologic stew is a rock called *serpentinite*. It is a slick, often shiny green to black rock that originates in the earth's upper mantle.

Granitic intrusions similar to the Wallowa batholith are scattered throughout the Baker terrane. The major plutons are the Bald Mountain batholith at the north end of the Elkhorn Mountains and Sunshine batholith in the Greenhorn Mountains. The granitic rocks that intrude the Baker terrane are similar in age, composition, and origin to the granitic rocks of the Wallowas. They range from 145 to 165 million years in age.

ELKHORN CREST TRAIL

Hike 47

ANTHONY LAKES TO MARBLE CANYON

Explore classic Baker terrane rocks and the gold-generating granitic rocks of the Bald Mountain batholith.

DISTANCE ■ **20 miles one way**

ELEVATION ■ **7,220 to 8,200 feet**

DIFFICULTY ■ **Moderate**

TOPOGRAPHIC MAPS ■ **Elkhorn Peak, Bourne, Mount Ireland, Anthony Lakes**

GEOLOGIC MAPS ■ **54–57**

PRECAUTIONS ■ A shuttle vehicle is required; at the Marble Canyon end, the road to the west looks enticing but is not maintained; it is steep and washboarded, and has several locations where slides and washouts are a hazard even to 4WD vehicles. The trail is usually open from late June to October.

FOR INFORMATION ■ **Baker Ranger District**

About the Landscape: The granitic rocks of the northern Elkhorn Mountains—mostly granodiorites—are cut by a multitude of parallel cracks called *joints.* The outcrops appear angular and broken. In a granite batholith, joints occur on large and small scales, cutting not only through mountaintops, but through microscopic mineral grains as well. The notches at the summits of Gunsight Mountain and Van Patten Peak are joints.

Two features typical of granodiorites occur in rock along the trail: dark blobs of the surrounding rock, assimilated into the batholith's hot magma, occur as irregular, rounded dark shapes called *xenoliths* (from the Greek *xeno* meaning "strange" and *lithos* meaning "rock"). Subtle layering is present also, especially in the light-colored granodiorite rocks in the Dutch Flat basin and along the base of Mount Ruth, several miles to the south. This layering develops as the magma cools, with darker minerals crystallizing and settling slowly into a layer, or being swept along magma channels and slowly deposited.

The thinly bedded sedimentary rocks abundant along the southern Elkhorn crest, including Elkhorn Peak, are a silica-rich sedimentary rock known as *chert.* Chert is a sedimentary rock that develops as the small, silica-rich skeletons of single-celled marine animals called *radiolarians* accumulate on the deep ocean floor. These skeletons partly dissolve and then solidify to form layer after layer of the 1-inch-thick chert beds. Microscopic radiolarian fossils can date the enclosing rock. According to fossil radiolaria, the Elkhorn Ridge *argillite* is mostly Triassic (about 220 to

230 million years in age), with a few older, Permian rocks. As in the rocks of the Wallowas and the Klamaths, fossils indicate that some older rocks of the Elkhorns (Baker terrane) came from an Asiatic sea.

Many old gold mines cluster near the contact between Baker terrane rocks and the Bald Mountain batholith. Gold was discovered near Auburn, on the south end of Elkhorn Ridge, in 1861, and gold mines flourished in the Elkhorn and Greenhorn Mountains from the early 1860s into the 1890s. The mines of the Bourne district, just west of the Elkhorn Crest Trail here, produced gold worth more than 150 million dollars. Several mines in this district were still active in the 1980s.

Trail Guide: To drop a shuttle vehicle at the south end of the trail, from Baker drive west on Pocahontas Road. Turn left onto Marble Canyon Road. The aptly named road tours past several limestone outcrops and through a limestone quarry that once supplied a large cement plant in Baker Valley. Technically this slightly recrystallized limestone is a marble. This road is easy and well graded for the first 5 miles, but it deteriorates as it rises steeply at about mile 6. Four-wheel-drive vehicles are recommended for the trip to the ridge crest at 7,400 feet, 15 miles from Baker. To reach the north trailhead at Anthony Lakes, from Baker drive north to Haines on

Argillite exposed in talus along Elkhorn Ridge

Twin Lakes in the Elkhorn Mountains

old Highway 30. Turn left (west) in Haines and take Elkhorn Scenic By-way (USFS Road 1146), following Anthony Lakes Ski Area signs, to Anthony Road and the well-marked trailhead parking area about 1 mile east of the ski area, about 30 miles from Baker.

From the Anthony Lakes trailhead, the Elkhorn Crest Trail goes south through lodgepole pine forest. This trail skirts Black Lake, a small, forest-choked glacial lake on the east side of Gunsight Mountain. The main Elkhorn Crest Trail climbs easily across granodiorite to the whitebark pine-laden passes above Antone and Dutch Flat Creeks, offering a distant view of the fault-controlled topography of the Grande Ronde valley 20 miles to the north. South of Dutch Flat Pass, at 6 miles a short trail leads east to Lost Lake, a good campsite and one of the few with water available along the high, dry Elkhorn Crest Trail.

From the junction with the Lost Lake trail, the Elkhorn Crest Trail skirts Mount Ruth. This peak wears a cap of fine-grained, light-colored granitic rock (*leucogranodiorite*) that is a slightly younger part of the large, composite

188

Bald Mountain batholith. In another mile, the trail crosses the contact between the Bald Mountain batholith's granitic rocks and the older rocks of the Baker terrane. This contact is abrupt. The *argillite*—a shale-like sedimentary rock—has been hardened and deformed. This effect is called contact metamorphism. As the trail continues south away from the batholith, the textures of the sedimentary rocks change to a more normal appearance.

The Elkhorn Crest Trail continues south across dark, deformed gabbro and greenstone of the Baker terrane. It also encounters several light-colored limestones and younger intrusive dikes. About 15 miles into the hike, the trail crosses the ridge between Rock Creek basin and the Twin Lakes basin. This cliff-infested area is a favorite hangout for Rocky Mountain goats. To the southwest, Twin Lakes provide a good camping site.

The Elkhorn Crest Trail continues another 5 miles across exposures of argillite to the Marble Canyon road and trailhead.

Hike 48

STRAWBERRY MOUNTAIN

SLIDE LAKE AND RABBIT EARS

Examine glacial lakes and the vents and flows of 6-million-year-old andesites.

DISTANCE ▪ **10 miles**

ELEVATION ▪ **5,773 to 8,172 feet**

DIFFICULTY ▪ **Strenuous**

TOPOGRAPHIC MAPS ▪ **Strawberry Mountain, Roberts Creek**

GEOLOGIC MAPS ▪ **58, 59**

PRECAUTIONS ▪ **The trail from Slide Lake to Rabbit Ears summit may be hazardous, especially early in the season, due to snow fields.**

FOR INFORMATION ▪ **Prairie City Ranger District**

Publisher's note: This area was extensively impacted by forest fires in 1996. Check with the ranger district before attempting this hike.

About the Landscape: The Strawberry volcanics are a Jekyll and Hyde range. The west half bares old rocks of the ancient arc, the east half young volcanics, about 16 million years in age. These young volcanic rocks erupted from vents in the east-central part of the range and spread east from John Day to Unity. They built at least one stratovolcano, centered just east of Strawberry Mountain. Strawberry Mountain itself was carved from the flanks of that larger peak by erosion, faulting, and glacial action.

Today, only the roots and lower flows of the old volcanos are left. Although contemporaries of the Columbia River basalts, the Strawberry volcanics are not directly related to Oregon's classic flood basalts.

Trail Guide: From US 26 in Prairie City, turn south on Main Street, left at the T intersection, and an immediate right onto Bridge Street (USFS Road 6001). Follow this road 11 miles to the Strawberry Lake campground and trailhead.

The trail to both Strawberry Lake and Slide Basin/Rabbit Ears begins on the east side of the campground. The broad, pleasant trail switchbacks up glacial headwalls and recessional moraines to a junction at 0.6 mile. (Take the trail to the right to explore around Strawberry Lake, a classic if elongate cirque. At the south end of the lake, a stunning panorama of layered basalt displays red layers of soils and cinders between flows. This area is accessible on trail 375-375A to Little Strawberry Lake. Just west of the layered andesite flows, a broad, yellow-gray cliff looms. This crumbly rock is the solidified vent through which the andesites erupted.)

From the junction at 0.6 mile, take trail 372 upslope to Rabbit Ears. The trail climbs through lodgepole and fir forest, and turns into Slide Basin— a classic U-shaped glacial valley. The valley wall above the trail and across the canyon is composed of andesite cliffs of the Strawberry volcanics. These rocks erupted from volcanic centers (like Rabbit Ears) here in the Strawberry Range. Along the trail many good examples of large, bulky andesite columns with thin, horizontal platy joints await your inspection.

Trail 372 to Rabbit Ears bypasses both the Big River Basin trail at 1.2 miles and the spur trail to Slide Lake (the trail number changes to trail 385 at the Slide Lake junction), and continues steadily upslope to the Slide Basin ridge line. The head of Slide Basin provides another excellent example of stacked basalt and andesite flows alternating with red soils and cinders.

The trail labors another 1.5 miles to the ridge. From the top of the ridge, the view of Rabbit Ears is almost anticlimactic. The vent for the major Strawberry Mountain eruption is smooth and a yellow-gray. Rabbit Ears, the pinnacles atop the ridge above High Lake, are composed of broken, oxidized rocks that define the side of the vent area. Note that Strawberry Mountain, in the background, is only a glacially sculpted pile of volcanic flows, and not a volcano in its own right. The rocks that compose Strawberry Mountain erupted here, at the Rabbit Ears vent, which once was part of a large volcano.

High Lake and Slide Lake provide camping sites, providing you have adequate water filtration or purification capacity. After you have explored the area, return as you came.

Crude columnar jointing is visible in Strawberry volcanics andesite along the trail to Slide Lake.

THE WESTERN BLUE MOUNTAINS

Things look different west of Picture Gorge. Sculpted cliffs mimic castles. Red-banded hills frame a sage-laden landscape. And sharp buttes poke at the sky. Today this is a stark, desertlike landscape, but the rocks hold tropical memories of magnolia and palm, of rhinos and tapirs and saber-toothed cats, and of ancient seas the ichthyosaur called home.

The western Blue Mountains reveal several significant scraps of the ancient arc. Just west of Mitchell the foundered remnants of a subduction zone lie in Meyers Canyon. These 225-million-year-old rocks are part of the Baker terrane. They include *blueschists*, a type of rock that develops at the very high pressures and low temperatures deep in a subduction zone.

The Cretaceous beach was near present-day Mitchell. After the Blue Mountains' island arc docked with North America, the Pacific shoreline

191

Sheep Rock is part of the John Day Fossil Beds National Monument.

ran just east of town. Layered conglomerates, sandstones, and shales, the sedimentary rocks west of Mitchell (the Gable Creek and Hudspeth Formations), were laid down just offshore. Wood chips and fish scales appear in the sandstones and shales along the highway. Fragments of an ichthyosaur, mosasaur (marine reptile), and pterosaur (avian reptile) have been reported from these rocks. The sandstones of the Hudspeth Formation yield spiraled-shelled ammonites in a few locations.

The buttes in the Mitchell basin mark the vents and magma chambers of long-vanished Clarno volcanos, 40 to 50 million years old. Clarno volcanoes resembled smaller, more tropical versions of the modern high Cascades.

The Painted Hills and John Day Fossil Beds National Monument showcase thick, colorful tuffs of the John Day Formation. Erupted between 39 and 25 million years ago, the John Day tuffs originated as ash erupted from the early (Western) Cascades. The ash was blown eastward by strong prevailing winds. No region in the world shows a more complete record of the plants and animals of the Tertiary period (50 to 5 million years ago) than the John Day basin. The extensive fossils preserve a record of profound climatic change in this area, from warm and wet 50 million years ago to present-day arid steppe environments.

Picture Gorge slices through a ridge west of Dayville. Its dark, layered walls reveal more than a dozen flows of basalt. These rocks are the Columbia River basalts' poor southern cousins, the Picture Gorge basalt. Erupted from vents near Monument, the Picture Gorge basalts are the same age (16 million years) and of similar composition as the Columbia River basalts. But they bear subtle differences in trace elements, a sort of geochemical DNA that distinguishes them as a distinct subspecies. Ash beds associated with the Picture Gorge basalts have produced a wealth of large mammalian fossils, including the Miocene ancestors of horses (six different genera), camels, bear, raccoons, rhinoceros, cats, dogs, and deer.

About 7.2 million years ago a huge caldera eruption shook the area near Burns. The eruption produced an ignimbrite that poured into the John Day basin at speeds of more than 100 mph and spread west, filling the John Day valley. The Rattlesnake ignimbrite forms the nearly horizontal cap on the ridge above Picture Gorge, and other chalky cliffs throughout the John Day basin. The vertebrate fossils found in the gravels above and below the Rattlesnake ignimbrite include the ancestors of dogs, lions, bears, camels, rhinos, and horses.

TWIN PILLARS

ANATOMY OF A 40-MILLION-YEAR-OLD VOLCANO

Explore the flanks and vent system of an Eocene volcano; visit Steins Pillar.

DISTANCE ■ **9 miles round trip**

ELEVATION ■ **3,737 to 5,542 to 3,737 feet**

DIFFICULTY ■ Moderate

TOPOGRAPHIC MAP ■ Steins Pillar

GEOLOGIC MAPS ■ 60, 61

PRECAUTIONS ■ In spring and other times of high water, the trail may be flooded or occupied by a creek side channel. Be prepared for wading. Also, changes in the channel have resulted in changes in trail location. Be aware that trail location and creek crossings may not be as mapped.

FOR INFORMATION ■ John Day Fossil Beds National Monument; Supervisor's Office, Ochoco National Forest

About the Landscape: The Ochoco Mountains are the westernmost range of the Blues. They showcase the Clarno Formation, the first volcanoes that erupted on Oregon's newly accreted land 40 to 50 million years ago. The

Steins Pillar, an erosional remnant of John Day formation tuffs, rises above Mill Creek.

Eocene climate was subtropical. Trees included avocado and palm. Animals included diminutive Eohippus ("dawn horse"), and primitive crocodiles. Broad plains occupied by wide, braided rivers separated the volcanoes. This Clarno landscape lay less than 70 miles from the coastline. Detailed information about Clarno paleontology can be found at the Cant Ranch Museum, John Day Fossil Beds National Monument (See Hike 50).

About 25 to 35 million years ago a new spasm of volcanic eruptions covered much of the Clarno landscape. These eruptions produced ash flow tuffs, rhyolites, and a few basalts. In eastern Oregon, these rocks are collectively known as the John Day formation.

Trail Guide: This hike leads into the throat of an eroded Clarno volcano. The vent conduit is now exposed as several tall pillars (Twin Pillars). Enroute to the trailhead, you can view the John Day formation in Steins Pillar.

From Prineville, drive east 9 miles on US Highway 26. Just beyond milepost 28, turn left (north) on Mill Creek Road. Mill Creek Road becomes USFS Road 33 at milepost 5. Follow the road 10.6 miles from Highway 26 to the trailhead at Wildcat Campground. Most outcrops and roadcuts along the wide valley are John Day rhyolites. For a brief side-trip to Steins Pillar—a 370-foot-high column of three John Day ash flow tuffs atop Clarno andesite, turn east (right) onto USFS Road 33-500 at 6.7 miles up Mill Creek Road, drive to the trailhead, and walk about 1 mile on trail 837 to the base of Steins Pillar.

From the Wildcat Campground trailhead, trail 380 leads up the narrow alluvial valley of East Fork, Mill Creek. This is a beautiful example of a braided stream, with well-developed channel complexity. The trail meanders up the valley, crossing and re-crossing the creek. The creek bottom displays angular cobbles of Clarno andesite, and more rounded, pink, banded rhyolite. The tawny-gray outcrops of Clarno andesite in the adjacent slopes once formed the flanks of the Twin Pillars volcano.

Two miles into the hike, the trail encounters narrow andesite outcrops that represent dikes that probably fed some Twin Pillar volcano eruptions. At about 2.5 miles, the trail, now on the east side of East Fork, Mill Creek (although the topo map shows it on the west) crosses Brogan Creek, and then ducks back to the west side of Mill Creek. This is an important crossing. Mill Creek is deeply incised into canyons as it works down through the softer ash and "vent agglomerate" of the volcanic throat. The best approach to Twin Pillars is along the trail as it works around a promontory on the creek's west side, and then crosses the creek, climbing and switchbacking upward 1,200 feet toward the base of Twin Pillars. The crumbling andesite and "vent agglomerate," a cemented accumulation of ash and angular rock fragments that filled the old volcanic conduit, are all that is left of Twin Pillar's vent system. Here, you are deep in an old volcanic throat, perhaps almost a mile below the original summit. Twin Pillars is the official turn-around. However, for dedicated rock collectors, the trail continues upward, leading to John Day rhyolite on the slopes above Twin Pillars.

195

BLUE BASIN LOOP

Hike 50

JOHN DAY FOSSIL BEDS

Loop through the Turtle Cove beds, home to Oligocene rhinos, bears, dogs, oreodonts, and, of course, turtles.

DISTANCE ■ 3-mile loop

ELEVATION ■ 2,490 to 3,000 feet

DIFFICULTY ■ Moderate

TOPOGRAPHIC MAPS ■ Clarno, Porcupine Butte

GEOLOGIC MAPS ■ 61, 62

PRECAUTIONS ■ Collecting fossils, or any other materials, in the national monument is illegal without a permit; permits are available only for research collection; you can inquire at the Cant Ranch headquarters about participating as a volunteer.

FOR INFORMATION ■ John Day Fossil Beds National Monument, Cant Ranch Headquarters

About the Landscape: The Blue Basin, named for the aquamarine color of the fragile tuff beds, is a deeply eroded badland circumnavigated and invaded by a developed trail. The bluish tuffs are 28.9 million years old

Banded Blue Basin tuffs

View into Blue Basin

(Oligocene). Like the rest of the John Day Formation in the western Blue Mountains, these tuffs were deposited as ash erupted from volcanos to the west and blown here by prevailing winds. The ash settled into shallow lakebeds. As did the remains of many large animals.

In this basin, pioneer paleontologist rivals Edward Cope and John Marsh collected fossils competitively in the 1870s. The fossils recovered here more recently include turtles, opossums, dogs, bear-dogs, bears, horses, rhinoceros, giant pigs, oreodonts, and mountain beaver, as well as a variety of rodents and a tiny animal known as a mouse-deer.

Trail Guide: From John Day, drive west on US 26 to Picture Gorge. Elegant exposures of the 16-million-year-old Picture Gorge basalt line the highway through the gorge; the ridge cut by Picture Gorge is capped by the 7.2-million-year-old Rattlesnake ignimbrite. In Picture Gorge, turn right on Highway 19 and cross the bridge over Rock Creek. A multilayered pinnacle known as Sheep Rock appears on the north side of the road 1 mile along Highway 19. Interpretive signs at the viewpoint explain Sheep Rock's geology. From this viewpoint, the Cant Ranch Interpretive Center is 0.2 mile farther on the north side of the road. To reach the trailhead, continue 4 miles west on Highway 19 to the Blue Basin turnoff and trailhead.

The loop trail around Blue Basin is easiest if hiked clockwise. Begin along the trail to the left that skirts the grassy backslope of the basin. The trail leads to sculpted cliffs on the east side of the basin, and after 1 mile climbs for a prolonged overview as it navigates the top of the basin.

The gravel trail finally descends steeply to the interior of the Blue Basin. Turn right along the paved side path to explore the badlands topography. This 0.5-mile portion of the trail leads into the interior of the Blue Basin. Several large fossils, including a turtle and an oreodont, are preserved in place and identified along the trail. Interpretive signs explain the rocks and the processes of fossil preservation and fossil discovery. Return to the main trail and the trailhead.

THE PAINTED HILLS

Hike 51

COLORFUL CLAYS

Four very short hikes explore the features and fossils of a colorful badlands.

DISTANCE ■ 3 miles

ELEVATION ■ 2,060 to 2,200 feet

DIFFICULTY ■ Easy to moderate

TOPOGRAPHIC MAPS ■ Sutton Mountain, Painted Hills

GEOLOGIC MAPS ■ 60–62

PRECAUTIONS ■ Park regulations forbid pedestrian traffic (or vehicles) except on developed trails; do not walk on other surfaces.

FOR INFORMATION ■ John Day Fossil Beds National Monument

About the Landscape: The Painted Hills look like enormous yellow- and red-striped piles of dirt. And they are. But it is very old dirt, mixed with volcanic ash. Beneath the soft exterior lies much harder bedrock. The rocks of the Painted Hills are Oligocene in age, about 25 to 39 million years old. They are part of the John Day Formation, an accumulation of volcanic ash from the Western Cascades. When this ash fell, it gradually began to support plants, and gradually turned into soil. Today, the bands in the Painted Hills mark ancient soil horizons.

Trail Guide: To reach the Painted Hills Unit, take US 26 to Mitchell. Continue 5 miles west of Mitchell and turn north on Bridge Creek Road. A well-preserved woolly mammoth tusk was found in the stream bank along Bridge Creek about 1.2 miles downstream from the road junction. Follow the Bridge Creek road 6 miles to the end of the pavement, and turn west (left) onto the gravel entrance road to the Painted Hills Unit. Drive past the picnic area to the overview. The first trails begin here.

The 0.5-mile round-trip Overlook Trail leads to an overview of the Big Basin tuff. The Painted Hills are composed of siltstones, accumulations of volcanic ash deposited in shallow lakebeds. The textured surface of the Painted Hills is composed of highly expandable clays that weather quickly from the solid ash-rich stone beneath. These clays absorb water so thoroughly that the clay literally out-competes plants for water. Not even a cactus can survive on the hill's unshaded, popcorn-textured surface. The

The surface of the Painted Hills is popcorn-textured.

red bands in the Painted Hills are sedimentary layers and old soil horizons that incorporated iron-rich clays from adjacent Clarno Formation rocks. Most black streaks are local concentrations of manganese oxide; a few are organic material—mostly lignite.

The 1.5-mile round-trip Carroll Rim Trail leads to an overview of the Painted Hills region. The trail climbs slopes of John Day tuff (the Turtle Cove member) and emerges atop the resistant ash-flow tuff (ignimbrite) at the Carroll Rim summit. This hard rock is the Picture Gorge ignimbrite, dated at 28.7 million years. (Note that this is *not* related to the Rattlesnake ignimbrite, 7.2 million years in age, that lies atop Picture Gorge!) To the east, Sutton Mountain is John Day tuff capped by Columbia River basalt. The top of Carroll Rim and the surrounding colorful soft sediment are in the John Day Formation. And to the north and west, the older Clarno Formation supports rugged hills.

The 0.3-mile loop Painted Cove trail provides an intimate view of the popcorn textures and intensely colored beds of the Painted Hills. Halfway around the flat loop, a John Day Formation rhyolite flow juts from an eroded slope.

The 0.3-mile round-trip Leaf Hill trail exposes a classic leaf-fossil collecting locality. The tuffs and lakebed sediments of the Painted Hills have yielded 107 species of leaves and 64 species of coniferous trees and herbaceous plants. The plants include maple, walnut, alder, beech, mulberry, elm, sycamore, hawthorne, metasequoia, pine, fir, hydrangea, pea, and fern. Animal fossils from this area include caddis flies, frogs, salamanders, fish, and a bat.

Geologic Time Chart

Era	Period	Epoch	Millions of Years Before the Present
Cenozoic	Quaternary	Holocene	
			0.01
		Pleistocene	
			1.6
	Tertiary	Pliocene	
			5.0
		Miocene	
			23
		Oligocene	
			35
		Eocene	
			57
		Paleocene	
			65
Mesozoic	Cretaceous		
			146
	Jurassic		
			208
	Triassic		
			245
Paleozoic	Permian		
			290
	Pennsylvanian		
			323
	Mississippian		
			363
	Devonian		
			409
	Silurian		
			439
	Ordovician		
			510
	Cambrian		
			570
Precambrian			

Glossary

aa—Hawaiian term for lavas that cool with broken or fractured pieces on their surface

amphibole—a dark, iron- or magnesium-rich silicate mineral usually rectangular or elongate in outline

amphibolite—a dark metamorphic rock containing the mineral amphibole; develops under very high temperatures and pressures

andesite—a volcanic igneous rock intermediate between basalt and rhyolite, usually gray, named after the Andes volcanos

argillite—a brittle, silica-rich, shale-like sedimentary rock, related to chert

basalt—a dark-colored, iron-rich volcanic igneous rock that contains pyroxene, olivine, and feldspar

batholith—a body of cooled plutonic rock greater than 100 square kilometers in area

bedding—the layers in which rock, especially sedimentary rock, is deposited

biotite—a dark, iron-rich silicate mineral, usually easily separated into paper-thin layers

biscuit mound (or biscuit scabland)—rough topography characterized by fine-grained silt mounds in a network of coarser stones or gravel

blueschist—a faintly blue-colored metamorphic rock that develops under conditions of very high pressure and low temperature

breccia—a rock composed of angular fragments of rock cemented or bonded together; usually created by explosions, rapid cooling, or movement along a fault

caldera—(1) a large basin-shaped depression in a volcanic summit, usually related to explosion; (2) a large, flat type of volcano that erupts explosive ash flows

chert—a sedimentary rock that develops as the small, silica-rich skeletons of single-celled marine animals called radiolarians accumulate on the deep ocean floor

cirque—a basin-shaped depression carved by ice at the head of a glacier

dacite—a light-colored volcanic igneous rock similar to andesite, with low magnesium, iron, and potassium contents; extrusive equivalent of granodiorite

dikes—narrow intrusions of magma that cut across bedding or layering in rock; feeder dikes serve as conduits of magma to surface eruptions

diorite—a gray-colored plutonic igneous rock intermediate between granite and gabbro, which looks like granite but contains less quartz; diorite usually contains the mineral amphibole or hornblende

dome—a bulbous accumulation, at a vent, of lava too viscous to flow

fault—physical break in the rock where one portion of the earth's crust has moved past another

feldspar—a white or gray silicate mineral composed of silica, aluminum, and some calcium, sodium, and/or potassium; most abundant component of igneous rocks

fold—bends or warped layering in rocks; the result of compression sometime in the rock's history

fumaroles—vents, often in the form of pipes or conduits through which hot gases trapped in an ash flow rise to the surface

gabbro—a dark-colored, iron-rich plutonic igneous rock, the intrusive equivalent of basalt

gneiss—a dark, hard, metamorphic rock that displays banding

graben—a valley or depression bounded and created by faulting

granite—a plutonic igneous rock which tends to be light in color, has a high content of quartz and potassium-rich feldspar, and often contains the dark mineral biotite

granitic, or granitoid, rock—a granite look-alike which may have a mineral composition different from granite

granodiorite—an intrusive igneous rock with less quartz and more feldspar than a "true" granite

greenstone—a catch-all term for gently metamorphosed basalt or other igneous rock that contains the minerals chlorite or epidote and has a greenish color

gutters—lava flow paths or channels

hornblende—a dark, hard, iron-rich mineral of the amphibole family; common in intermediate igneous rocks including diorite and andesite; often appears as shiny black rectangles

igneous rock—rock formed when lava or magma cools

ignimbrite—tuff or welded tuff that erupts in glowing clouds, moves at high speed, and solidifies into a hard, glassy but porous rock

intrusion—an emplacement of molten rock in already existing rock

island arc—a linear chain of volcanic islands that develops above a subduction zone

joints—cracks or separations along which there has been no movement; related to cooling or stress. *Compare* **fault**

lahars—volcanic mudflows, usually hot

lava—fluid, molten rock that flows on the surface; magma that has erupted

lava bomb—*See* **volcanic bomb**

maar—a crater left after volcanic explosions that produced only gas rather than a lava eruption

magma—fluid, molten rock beneath the earth's surface

mantle—the main bulk of the earth, 25 to 1,800 miles deep, which lies between the core and the crust; composed of peridotite; rocks from the mantle may be faulted or carried to the surface when continents collide with island arcs or another continent

marble—heated, recrystallized limestone; a metamorphic rock

melange—a zone of mixed or different rocks held in a matrix of shale or serpentinite; usually associated with subduction zones

metamorphic rock—any rock changed from its original form by heat and/or pressure

moraine—unsorted gravels transported and deposited at the margin of a glacier

obsidian—a glassy form of rhyolite or dacite

olivine—an olive green silicate mineral high in magnesium and iron that occurs in basalt and is abundant in peridotite

pahoehoe—Hawaiian term for a basalt lava flow with a smooth, ropy, and often glassy surface

peridotite—dense, magnesium-rich rock that composes the earth's mantle; on the surface, peridotite weathers to a bright reddish brown

pillow lava—molten lava, usually basalt, that chilled and solidified very quickly under water, resulting in globby forms and glassy exterior

pluton—a massive, dome-shaped intrusion of igneous rock

plutonic (or intrusive) rock—rocks formed if a lava never reaches the surface and cools slowly underground

pumice—porous, silica-rich volcanic glass produced in explosive eruptions; related to rhyolite and obsidian; may float

pyroxene—a dark, iron- and magnesium-rich silicate mineral common in basalt and gabbro; usually very small and fine-grained

quartz—silicon dioxide; one of the most abundant rock-forming minerals; colored forms include amethyst (purple) and rose quartz (pink)

rhyodacite—a fine-grained, light-colored volcanic rock; extrusive equivalent of granodiorite

rhyolite—a quartz- and potassium-feldspar-rich, light-colored volcanic igneous rock; the extrusive equivalent of granite; often banded; may contain biotite

sandstone—sedimentary rock composed of sand-sized particles

schist—a fragile metamorphic rock that develops thin layers of mica and other shiny minerals

scoria—oxidized, red-colored volcanic cinders

seafloor spreading—opening of the ocean floor at mid-ocean ridges; part of the plate tectonic process

seamounts—submarine volcanos related to a stationary source of magma in the earth's mantle (a hotspot) rather than to a subduction zone

sedimentary rock—rocks deposited in layers by water or wind

serpentinite—metamorphosed periodite, usually shiny green or black

shale—fine-grained sedimentary rock composed of silt and clay

shield volcano—a broad volcano with gentle slopes that erupts fluid basalt

sill—a flat-topped and flat-bottomed intrusion running parallel to bedding layers

stratovolcano—a volcano composed of layers of ash and lava

striations—grooves worn by glacial ice or by rocks carried in ice

subduction—the process by which the seafloor is pushed and pulled down into the earth's mantle

subduction zone—the slanting zone where the seafloor plunges back down into the earth's mantle

terminal moraine—unsorted gravel that a glacier piles at its far or terminal end

terrane—a group of rock formations formed by similar or related processes over an extended time; often transported and added to a continent by plate tectonic processes

tonalite—a plutonic igneous rock with less quartz and more calcium-rich feldspar than a "true" granite; closely resembles granite in appearance

tsunami—tidal wave generated by an offshore earthquake

tuff—volcanic ash compressed into rock

vesicle—a cavity, usually small, formed by the entrapment of gas as a lava cools; found in volcanic igneous rocks

volcanic bomb—a blob of lava that was ejected while viscous and became rounded while in flight

volcanic (or **extrusive**) **rock**—rocks formed when lava erupts and solidifies

welded tuff—rock formed when very hot, nearly molten particles of ash stick or weld together

xenoliths—an inclusion of foreign rock in an igneous body; from the Greek *xeno*, "strange," and *lithos*, "rock"

Recommended Reading

Allen, John Eliot. *The Magnificent Gateway.* Portland, Ore.: Timber Press, 1979.

Allen, John Eliot, Marjorie Burns, and Sam C. Sargent. *Cataclysms on the Columbia.* Portland, Ore.: Timber Press, 1986.

Bishop, E. M. "The Mystery of the OWL." *Earth Magazine* 2 (1993): 58–63.

Brogan, Phil. *East of the Cascades.* Portland, Ore.: Binford and Mort, 1965.

Compton, Robert. *Geology in the Field.* New York: John Wiley, 1985.

Cvancara, Alan M. *A Field Manual for the Amateur Geologist.* New York: Prentice Hall, 1985.

Dixon, Dougal, and Raymond Bernor. *The Practical Geologist.* New York: Simon and Schuster, 1992.

Fry, Norman. *The Field Description of Metamorphic Rocks.* London: The Open University Press, 1984.

Harris, Stephen L. *Fire Mountains of the West.* Missoula, Mont.: Mountain Press, 1988.

Lahee, Frederick. *Field Geology.* New York: McGraw Hill, 1980.

McPhee, John. *Assembling California.* New York: Farrar Straus Giroux, 1991.

———. *Basin and Range.* New York: Farrar Straus Giroux, 1986.

———. *In Suspect Terrain.* New York: Farrar Straus Giroux, 1983.

Orr, Elizabeth, and William Orr. *Geology of the Pacific Northwest.* New York: McGraw Hill, 1995.

———. *Rivers of the West.* Salem, Ore.: Eagle Web Press, 1985.

Orr, Elizabeth, William Orr, and Ewart Baldwin. *Geology of Oregon.* Dubuque, Iowa: Kendall Hunt, 1992.

Potter, Miles. *Oregon's Golden Years.* Caldwell, Idaho: Caxton, 1976.

Press, Frank, and Raymond Siever. *Understanding Earth.* New York: W. H. Freeman, 1994.

Reyes, Chris, ed. *The Table Rocks of Jackson County: Islands in the Sky.* Ashland, Ore.: Last Minute Publications, 1994.

Stanley, G. D. "Travels of an Ancient Reef." *Natural History* 87 (1986): 36–42.

Thorpe and Brown. *The Field Description of Igneous Rocks.* London: The Open University Press, 1985.

Tucker, Gerald. *The Story of Hells Canyon.* Sheep Creek Publishing, 1993.

Tucker, Maurice. *The Field Description of Sedimentary Rocks.* London: The Open University Press, 1982.

Wallace, David Rains. *The Klamath Knot.* San Francisco: Sierra Club Books, 1983.

Williams, Ira A. *Geologic History of the Columbia River Gorge.* 1923. Reprint, Portland, Ore.: Oregon Historical Society, 1991.

Appendix A. Geologic Maps

1. Geologic map of Oregon. G. Walker and N. McLeod. USGS, 1991. 1:500,000.

CHAPTER 1. THE KLAMATH MOUNTAINS

2. Preliminary geologic map of the Eagle Point and Sams Valley quadrangles, Jackson County, Oregon. T. J. Wiley and J. G. Smith. Oregon Dept. Geology and Mineral Industries, Open File Report O-93-13. 1993.
3. Geologic map of the Kalmiopsis Wilderness, southwestern Oregon. N. J. Page et al. USGS, Map MF-1240-A. 1981. 1:62,500.
4. Mineral resource potential, Kalmiopsis Wilderness, southwestern Oregon. N. J. Page and M. S. Miller. USGS, Map MF-1240-E. 1981. 1:62,500.
5. Preliminary geologic map of the Medford 1x2 degree sheet. J. G. Smith et al. USGS, Open File Report O-82-955. 1982. 1:250,000.
6. Lode gold characteristics of the Medford 1x2 degree quadrangle. N. J. Page et al. USGS, Map MF-1383-D. 1983. 1:250,000.
7. Geologic map of the Wild Rogue Wilderness, Coos, Curry, and Douglas Counties, Oregon. F. Gray et al. USGS, Map MF-1381-A. 1982. 1:48,000.
8. Geology of the south half of the Coos Bay 2 degree sheet. M. L. Blake, Jr. and A. S. Jayco. USGS, Open File Map. 1989.

CHAPTER 2. THE COAST RANGE

9. Geology of the Marys Peak and Alsea quadrangles, Oregon. E. Baldwin. USGS, Map OM-162. 1955. 1:62,500.
10. Geology and mineral resources of Coos County, Oregon. E. Baldwin et al. Oregon Dept. Geology and Mineral Industries, Bulletin 80. 1973. 1:62,500

CHAPTER 3. THE WILLAMETTE VALLEY

11. Geologic map of the Drake Crossing 7.5' quadrangle, Marion County, Oregon. Oregon Dept. Geology and Mineral Industries, GMS-50.

12. Geologic map of Elk Prairie 7.5' quadrangle, Marion and Clackamas Counties. Oregon Dept. Geology and Mineral Industries, GMS-51.

13. Geologic map of the Lake Oswego quadrangle, Clackamas, Multnomah, and Washington Counties, Oregon. M. H. Beeson et al. Oregon Dept. Geology and Mineral Industries, GMS-59. 1989. 1:24,000.

14. Geologic map of the Damascas quadrangle, Clackamas and Multnomah Counties, Oregon. I. P. Madin. Oregon Dept. Geology and Mineral Industries, GMS-60. 1994. 1:24,000.

15. Geologic map of the Portland quadrangle, Multnomah and Washington Counties, Oregon, and Clark County, Washington. M. H. Beeson et al. Oregon Dept. Geology and Mineral Industries, GMS-75. 1991. 1:24,000.

16. Earthquake hazard map of the Portland quadrangle, Multnomah and Washington Counties, Oregon, and Clark County, Washington. M. A. Mabey et al. Oregon Dept. Geology and Mineral Industries, GMS-79.

17. Earthquake hazard map of the Mount Tabor quadrangle, Clackamas, Multnomah, and Washington Counties, Oregon. Oregon Dept. Geology and Mineral Industries, GMS-89. 1995. 1:24,000.

18. Earthquake hazard map of the Beaverton quadrangle, Oregon. Oregon Dept. Geology and Mineral Industries, GMS-90. 1994. 1:24,000.

19. Earthquake hazard map of the Lake Oswego quadrangle, Clackamas, Multnomah, and Washington Counties, Oregon. Oregon Dept. Geology and Mineral Industries, GMS-91. 1994. 1:24,000.

20. Earthquake hazard map of the Gladstone quadrangle, Clackamas, Multnomah, and Washington Counties, Oregon. Oregon Dept. Geology and Mineral Industries, GMS-92. 1995. 1:24,000.

CHAPTER 4. THE COLUMBIA RIVER GORGE

21. Geologic and neotectonic evaluation of North-central Oregon: The Dalles 1x2 degree quadrangle. James Bella. Oregon Dept. Geology and Mineral Industries, GMS-27. 1982. 1:250,000.

CHAPTER 5. THE CASCADES

22. Geologic map of the Mount Hood Wilderness, Clackamas and Hood River Counties, Oregon. T. E. C. Keith et al. USGS, Map MF-1379A. 1982. 1:62,500.

23. Geothermal investigations in the vicinity of the Mount Hood Wilderness, Clackamas and Hood River Counties, Oregon. J. H. Robison et al. USGS, Map MF-1379 B. 1982.

24. Geology of the Mount Hood volcano. W. S. Wise. In: Andesite

Conference Guidebook, H. Dole, ed. Oregon Dept. Geology and Mineral Industries, Bulletin 62. 1968.

25. Geologic map of Oregon. Oregon Dept. Geology and Mineral Industries. 1991, 1:500,000.

26. Geology of Mount Jefferson. Richard Conrey. Washington State University Ph.D., unpublished. 1990. 1:62,500.

27. Geologic map of the Three Sisters Wilderness, Deschutes, Lane, and Linn Counties, Oregon. E. M. Taylor et al. USGS, Map MF-1952. 1987. 1:63,360.

28. Geologic map of the Mount Bachelor Chain and surrounding area. W. E. Scott and C. A. Gardner. USGS, Map I-1967. 1992. 1:50,000.

29. Field geology of SW Broken Top quadrangle, Oregon. E. M. Taylor. Oregon Dept. Geology and Mineral Industries, Special Paper 2. 1978.

30. Roadside Geology of the Santiam Pass Area. E. M. Taylor. In: Andesite Conference Guidebook, Oregon Dept. Geology and Mineral Industries, Bulletin 62. 1968.

31. Aeromagnetic and Gravity Surveys of the Crater Lake region, Oregon [Geology of Crater Lake]. H. Richard Blank. In: Andesite Conference Guidebook, H. Dole, ed. Oregon Dept. Geology and Mineral Industries, Bulletin 62. 1968.

CHAPTER 6. THE DESCHUTES BASIN

32. Geologic map of the Eagle Butte and Gateway quadrangles, Jefferson and Wasco Counties, Oregon. G. A. Smith and G. A. Hayman. Oregon Dept. Geology and Mineral Industries, GMS-43. 1987. 1:24,000.

33. Geologic map of the Seekseequa Junction and a portion of the Metolius Bench quadrangles, Jefferson County, Oregon. G. A. Smith. Oregon Dept. Geology and Mineral Industries, GMS-44. 1987. 1:24,000.

34. Geologic map of the Madras East and Madras West quadrangles. G. A. Smith. Oregon Dept. Geology and Mineral Industries, GMS-45. 1987. 1:24,000.

35. Geologic map of the Smith Rock area, Jefferson, Deschutes, and Crook Counties, Oregon. P.T. Robinson and D.H. Stensland. USGS, Map I1142. 1979.1:48,000.

CHAPTER 7. THE HIGH LAVA PLAINS

36. Geologic map of Newberry Volcano, Deschutes, Klamath, and Lake Counties, Oregon. USGS, Map MI-2455. 1995. 1:62,500 and 1:24,000

37. Roadside Guide to the Geology of Newberry Volcano. R. A. Jensen. Cen. Ore. Geo. Pub. 1995.

38. Reconnaissance geologic map of the west half of the Bend and the east half of the Shelvin Park 7.5' quadrangles, Deschutes County, Oregon. USGS, MF-2189. 1:24,000.

CHAPTER 8. THE BASIN AND RANGE

39. Geologic map of the High Steens and Little Blitzen Gorge Wilderness Study Areas, Harney County, Oregon. Scott Minor et al. USGS, Misc. Field Studies Map MF-1876. 1987.
40. Geologic map of the Wildhorse Lake quadrangle, Harney County, Oregon. Scott A. Minor et al. USGS, Misc. Field Studies Map MF-1915. 1987.
41. Geologic map of the Alvord Hot Springs quadrangle, Harney County, Oregon. Scott A. Minor et al. USGS, Misc. Field Studies Map MF-1916. 1987.
42. Geologic map of the Krumbo Reservoir quadrangle, Harney County, Southeastern Oregon. J. A. Johnson. USGS, Misc. Field Studies Map MF-2267. 1994.
43. Mineral resources of the Pueblo Mountains Wilderness Study Area, Harney County, Oregon, and Humbolt County, Nevada. Roback et al. USGS, Bulletin 1740B. 1987.

CHAPTER 9. THE OWYHEES

44. Preliminary geologic map of the Three Fingers Rock quadrangle, Malheur County, Oregon. D. B. Vander et al. USGS, Open File Report O-89-334. 1989. 1:24,000.
45. Geologic map of the Pelican Point quadrangle, Malheur County, Oregon. D. B. Vander Meulen et al. USGS, Misc. Field Studies Map MF-1904. 1987. 1:24,000.
46. Geologic map of the Rooster Comb quadrangle, Malheur County, Oregon. D. B. Vander Meulen et al. USGS, Misc. Field Studies Map MF-1902. 1987. 1:24,000.
47. Geology and mineral resources of the Grassy Mountain quadrangle, Malheur County, Oregon. M. L. Ferns and L. Ramp. Oregon Dept. Geology and Mineral Industries, GMS-57. 1989. 1:24,000.
48. Geologic map of the Owyhee Canyon Wilderness Study Area, Malheur County, Oregon. James G. Evans. USGS, Misc. Field Studies Map MF-1926. 1987. 1:62,500.
49. Geologic map of the Lower Owyhee Canyon Wilderness Study Area, Malheur County, Oregon. James G. Evans. USGS, Misc. Field Studies Map MF-2167. 1991. 1:48,000.
50. Geologic map of the Mahogany Mountain 30x60 minute quadrangle, Malheur County, Oregon and Owyhee County, Idaho. Mark

L. Ferns et al. Oregon Dept. Geology and Mineral Industries, GMS-78. 1993. 1:100,000.

51. Geologic map of the Vale 30x60 minute quadrangle, Malheur County, Oregon and Owyhee County, Idaho. Mark L. Ferns et al. Oregon Dept. Geology and Mineral Industries, GMS-77. 1993. 1:100,000.

CHAPTER 10. THE BLUE MOUNTAINS

52. Geologic map of the Snake River Canyon, Oregon and Idaho. In: A Preliminary Report on the geology of part of the Snake River Canyon, Oregon and Idaho. T. L. Vallier. Oregon Dept. Geology and Mineral Industries, GMS-6. 1974.

53. Reconnaissance geology of the Wallowa Lake quadrangle. In: Geology and Physiography of the Northern Wallowa Mountains, Oregon. W. D. Smith and J. E. Allen. Oregon Dept. Geology and Mineral Industries, Bulletin 12. 1941. Approx. 1:100,000.

54. Reconnaissance geologic map of the Oregon part of the Grangeville quadrangle, Baker, Union, Umatilla, and Wallowa Counties, Oregon. G. Walker. USGS, MI-1116. 1979.

55. Geology and gold deposits of the Bourne quadrangle, Baker and Grant Counties, Oregon. H. C. Brooks et al. Oregon Dept. Geology and Mineral Industries, GMS-19. 1982. 1:24,000.

56. Geology and mineral resources map of the Elkhorn Peak quadrangle, Baker County, Oregon. M. L. Ferns. Oregon Dept. Geology and Mineral Industries, GMS-41. 1987. 1:24,000.

57. Geology and mineral resources map of the Mt. Ireland quadrangle, Baker and Grant Counties, Oregon. M. L. Ferns et al. Oregon Dept. Geology and Mineral Industries, GMS-22. 1982.

58. Geology of the Canyon City quadrangle, northeastern Oregon. T. P. Thayer and C. E. Brown. USGS, Misc. Investigations Map MI-447. 1966.

59. Mineral resources of the Strawberry Mountain Wilderness and adjacent areas, Grant County, Oregon. T. P. Thayer et al. USGS, Bulletin 1498. 1981.

60. Reconnaissance geologic map of the east half of the Bend quadrangle, Crook, Wheeler, Jefferson, Wasco, and Deschutes Counties, Oregon. D. A. Swanson. USGS, Misc. Investigations Map MI-568. 1969. 1:250,000.

61. Reconnaissance geologic map of the John Day Formation in the southwestern part of the Blue Mountains and adjacent areas, north-central Oregon. P. T. Robinson. USGS, Misc. Investigations Map MI-872. 1975. 1:125,000.

62. John Day Basin Paleontology Field Trip Guide and Road Log. T. Fremd et al. Society of Vertebrate Paleontology. 1994. Variable scales.

Appendix B. Addresses

Alsea Ranger District (USFS), 18591 Alsea Highway, Alsea, OR 97324; (541) 487-5811

Ashland Ranger District (USFS), 645 Washington Street, Ashland, OR 97520; (541) 482-3333

Baker Ranger District (USFS), 3165 Tenth Street, Baker City, OR 97814; (541) 523-4476

Bend Ranger District (USFS), 1230 NE Third, Bend, OR 97701; (541) 388-5664

Burns District (BLM), HC 74, 12533 Highway 20 West, Hines, OR 97738; (541) 573-4400

Cape Arago State Park, c/o Oregon State Parks Regional Office, 365 North Fourth Street, Suite A, Coos Bay, OR 97420; (541) 269-9410

Cape Lookout State Park, c/o Oregon State Parks Regional Office, 416 Pacific Street, Tillamook, OR 97141; (541) 842-5501

Chetco Ranger District (USFS), 555 Fifth Street, Brookings, OR 97415; (541) 469-2196

Columbia Gorge Ranger District (USFS), 31520 SE Woodard Road, Troutdale, OR 97060; (503) 695-2276

Cove Palisades State Park, 44300 Jordan Road, Culver, OR 97734; (541) 546-3412

Crater Lake National Park, P.O. Box 128, Crater Lake, OR 97604; (541) 594-2211

Eagle Cap Ranger District (USFS), 88401 Highway 82, Enterprise, OR 97828; (541) 426-4978

Fort Rock Ranger District (USFS), 1230 NE Third, Bend, OR 97701; (541) 388-5674

Fort Rock State Park, c/o Oregon State Parks Regional Office, P.O. Box 5309, Bend, OR 97708; (541) 388-6211

Guy W. Talbot State Park, c/o Oregon State Parks Regional Office, 3554 SE 82nd Avenue, Portland, OR 97266; (503) 238-7491

Hells Canyon National Recreation Area, 88401 Highway 82, Enterprise, OR 97828; (541) 426-4978

Hood River Ranger District (USFS), 6780 Highway 35 South, Hood River, OR 97041; (541) 352-6002

John Day Fossil Beds National Monument, 420 West Main Street, John Day, OR 97845; (541) 575-0721

John Day Fossil Beds National Monument, Cant Ranch Headquarters, Dayville, OR 97825; (541) 987-2333

Lane County Parks Division, 3040 North Delta Highway, Eugene, OR 97401; (541) 341-6900

La Pine State Recreation Area, c/o Oregon State Parks Regional Office, P.O. Box 5309, Bend, OR 97708; (541) 388-6211

McKenzie Ranger District (USFS), McKenzie Bridge, OR 97413; (541) 822-3381

Medford District (BLM), 3040 Biddle Road, Medford, OR, 97504; (541) 770-2200

The Nature Conservancy, 1234 NW 25th Street, Portland, OR 97828; (503) 228-9561

Nature of Oregon Information Center, 800 NE Oregon Street, Portland, OR 97232; (503) 731-4444

Newberry National Volcanic Monument, Deschutes National Forest, 1230 NE Third, Bend, OR 97701 (541) 388-5674

Ochoco National Forest, Supervisor's Office, P.O. Box 490, 3160 NE Third Street, Prineville, OR 97754; (541) 416-6500

Oregon Caves National Monument, Cave Junction, OR 97523; (541) 592-3400

Oregon Department of Geology and Mineral Industries, 800 NE Oregon Street, Suite 941, Portland, OR 97232; (503) 731-4100

Oregon Dunes National Recreation Area, Siuslaw National Forest, 855 Highway Avenue, Reedsport, OR 97467; (541) 271-3611

Oregon Museum of Science and Industry, 1945 SE Water Avenue, Portland, OR 97214; (503) 797-4545

Portland Parks and Recreation Department, Hoyt Arboretum, 4000 SW Fairview Boulevard, Portland, OR 97221; (503) 823-3655

Prairie City Ranger District (USFS), 327 Front Street, Prairie City, OR 97869; (541) 820-3311

Saddle Mountain State Park, c/o Oregon State Parks Regional Office, 416 Pacific Street, Tillamook, OR 97141; (541) 842-5501

Salem District (BLM), 1717 Fabry Road SE, Salem, OR 97306; (503) 375-5646

Shore Acres State Park, c/o Oregon State Parks Regional Office, 365 North Fourth Street, Suite A, Coos Bay, OR 97420; (541) 269-9410

Silver Falls State Park, c/o Oregon State Parks and Recreation Division, 525 Trade Street SE, Salem, OR 97310; (503) 378-6305

Siskiyou National Forest, 200 NE Greenfield Road, P.O. Box 440, Grants Pass, OR 97526; (541)479-5301

Sisters Ranger District (USFS), P.O. Box 249, Highway 20, Sisters, OR, 97759; (541) 549-2111

Smith Rock State Park, c/o Oregon State Parks Regional Office, P.O. Box 5309, Bend, OR 97708; (541) 388-6211

Sunset Bay State Park, c/o Oregon State Parks Regional Office, 365 North Fourth Street, Suite A, Coos Bay, OR 97420; (541) 269-9410

Tahkenitch Lake State Park, c/o Oregon State Parks Regional Office, 365 North Fourth Street, Suite A, Coos Bay, OR 97420; (541) 269-9410

US Forest Service, Region Six Headquarters, Pacific Northwest Regional Office, 319 Pine Street, Portland, OR 97208; (503) 221-2877

USGS, Branch of Distribution/Information Center, Box 25286, Federal Center, Denver, CO 80225

Vale District (BLM), 100 Oregon Street, Vale, OR 97918;

Zigzag Ranger District (USFS), 70220 East Highway 26, Zigzag, OR 97049; (541) 622-3191

Index

ABOUT THE AUTHORS

ELLEN MORRIS BISHOP's interest in geology began early—at age six she was collecting rocks and sending fossils to the American Museum of Natural History for identification. A specialist in igneous petrology and the exotic terranes of eastern Oregon, she received her Ph.D. from Oregon State University in 1982. She has written a science column for the Portland *Oregonian* and currently teaches field-oriented geology and ecosystems courses as an adjunct professor at Lewis and Clark College in Portland. She also works as a documentary photographer and photojournalist. She lives in northeast Oregon with her husband David, five dogs, one Arabian mare, and a precocious cat named Rafter.

JOHN ELIOT ALLEN has mapped and hiked Oregon's geology from the Wallowas to the coast. In addition to his distinguished career in teaching and research at Portland State University, he is the author of two acclaimed books about the Columbia River Gorge as well as "Time Travel" columns for the *Oregonian*. He lives in Portland with his wife of 63 years, Peggy.

OTHER TITLES YOU MAY ENJOY
FROM THE MOUNTAINEERS

Exploring Oregon's Wild Areas: A Guide for Hikers, Backpackers, Climbers, X-C Skiers, & Paddlers (**2d Ed.**), William L. Sullivan
Revised and updated guide to state-wide wilderness areas, wildlife refuges, nature preserves, and state parks.

Exploring the Wild Oregon Coast, Bonnie Henderson
Guide to the best hiking, canoeing, bicycling, horseback riding, and wildlife watching spots along the Oregon Coast.

Oregon State Parks: A Complete Recreation Guide, Jan Bannan
Comprehensive guide to year-round activities in the state's parks for hikers, campers, whitewater rafters, picnickers, and other outdoor enthusiasts.

Cross-Country Ski Routes: Oregon, Klindt Vielbig
Guidebook to 500 trails with descriptions and maps for beginning to advanced tours.

Hiking the Great Northwest: The 55 Greatest Trails in Washington, Oregon, Idaho, Montana, Wyoming, British Columbia, Canadian Rockies, & Northern California, Ira Spring, Harvey Manning, & Vicky Spring
Complete guide to favorite Northwest day hikes and backpacks.

Day Hikes from Oregon Campgrounds, Rhonda & George Ostertag
Selected campgrounds throughout the state which access the best hikes and nature walks in Oregon.

50 Hikes in Oregon's Coast Range & Siskiyous, Rhonda & George Ostertag
Hikes in the mountain corridor between I-5 and Hwy. 101, from $1/2$-mile walks to 47-mile backpacks.

100 Hikes in Oregon, Rhonda & George Ostertag
Fully-detailed, best-selling hiking guide highlighting the best trails and sights in the Oregon wilderness.

Animal Tracks of the Pacific Northwest, Chris Stall
Tracks and information on 40 to 50 animals common to the region.

THE MOUNTAINEERS, founded in 1906, is a nonprofit outdoor activity and conservation club, whose mission is "to explore, study, preserve, and enjoy the natural beauty of the outdoors. . . . " Based in Seattle, Washington, the club is now the third-largest such organization in the United States, with 15,000 members and five branches throughout Washington State.

The Mountaineers sponsors both classes and year-round outdoor activities in the Pacific Northwest, which include hiking, mountain climbing, ski-touring, snowshoeing, bicycling, camping, kayaking and canoeing, nature study, sailing, and adventure travel. The club's conservation division supports environmental causes through educational activities, sponsoring legislation, and presenting informational programs. All club activities are led by skilled, experienced volunteers, who are dedicated to promoting safe and responsible enjoyment and preservation of the outdoors.

If you would like to participate in these organized outdoor activities or the club's programs, consider a membership in The Mountaineers. For information and an application, write or call The Mountaineers, Club Headquarters, 300 Third Avenue West, Seattle, WA 98119; (206) 284-6310.

The Mountaineers Books, an active, nonprofit publishing program of the club, produces guidebooks, instructional texts, historical works, natural history guides, and works on environmental conservation. All books produced by The Mountaineers are aimed at fulfilling the club's mission.

Send or call for our catalog of more than 300 outdoor titles:

The Mountaineers Books
1001 SW Klickitat Way, Suite 201
Seattle, WA 98134
1-800-553-4453/e-mail; mbooks@mountaineers.org